The Big Book of Behavior Management, K–5

The Big Book of Behavior Management, K–5

Positive, Proactive, Prosocial Interventions and Prevention Strategies

David Campos

Kathleen McConnell Fad

FOR INFORMATION:

Corwin
A SAGE Company
2455 Teller Road
Thousand Oaks, California 91320
(800) 233-9936
www.corwin.com

SAGE Publications Ltd.
1 Oliver's Yard
55 City Road
London EC1Y 1SP
United Kingdom

SAGE Publications India Pvt. Ltd.
Unit No 323-333, Third Floor, F-Block
International Trade Tower Nehru Place
New Delhi 110 019
India

SAGE Publications Asia-Pacific Pte. Ltd.
18 Cross Street #10-10/11/12
China Square Central
Singapore 048423

Associate Vice President and Editorial Director: Monica Eckman
Senior Publisher: Jessica Allan
Senior Content Development Editor: Mia Rodriguez
Project Editor: Amy Schroller
Copy Editor: Lynne Curry
Typesetter: C&M Digitals (P) Ltd.
Proofreader: Dennis Webb
Cover Designer: Candice Harman
Marketing Manager: Olivia Bartlett

Printed and bound by CPI Group (UK) Ltd, Croydon, CR0 4YY

Library of Congress Cataloging-in-Publication Data

Names: Campos, David, author. | McConnell, Kathleen, author.

Title: The big book of behavior management, K-5 : positive, proactive, prosocial interventions and prevention strategies / David Campos, Kathleen McConnell Fad.

Description: Thousand Oaks, California : Corwin, [2025] | Includes bibliographical references and index.

Identifiers: LCCN 2024057307 | ISBN 9781071981184 (paperback) | ISBN 9781071981191 (epub) | ISBN 9781071981214 (epub) | ISBN 9781071981221 (pdf)

Subjects: LCSH: Behavior modification. | Classroom management. | School children—Discipline. | Problem children—Behavior modification. | Elementary school teaching.

Classification: LCC LB1060.2 .C35 2025 | DDC 370.15/28—dc23eng/20250205

LC record available at https://lccn.loc.gov/2024057307

25 26 27 28 29 10 9 8 7 6 5 4 3 2 1

CONTENTS

COMPANION WEBSITE CONTENTS

Intervention 4: Talking/No Talking
- Talking/No Talking for Poster/Sign
- Talking/No Talking Voice Levels for Poster/Sign

Intervention 8: Work Zones
Intervention 11: What's Going On?
Intervention 18: How Am I Doing?
Intervention 22: Study Buddies
Intervention 27: Good News/Bad News
Intervention 35: Inside/Outside Circles
Intervention 44: Say No Silently
Intervention 47: De-Stress
- Signals of Stress List
- De-Stress Movements
- My Personal De-Stress Plan

For downloadable versions of these interventions, please visit our companion website.
https://companion.corwin.com/courses/BigBookofBehaviorManagementK5

ABOUT THE AUTHORS

David Campos began his career in education more than thirty years ago, when he started teaching second grade. He earned his PhD from The University of Texas at Austin, specializing in learning disabilities and behavior disorders. His scholarship focuses on instructional design and delivery, childhood health and wellness, and LGBTQ children and adolescents. He has written books on childhood loneliness, childhood obesity, and inspiring creativity in students, among others. He lives in San Antonio, Texas.

Kathleen McConnell Fad has a PhD in learning disabilities and behavior disorders from The University of Texas at Austin. Kathy was a general and special education teacher before working as a college professor and a consultant specializing in emotional and behavioral disorders. Her publications focus on practical strategies for teachers, counselors, and educational specialists. Kathy's most recent books, also coauthored with David Campos, provides teachers with important information and easy-to-use interventions for childhood loneliness and anxiety. She lives in Austin, Texas.

PART I

INTRODUCTION AND RATIONALE

INTRODUCTION

What's in This Chapter

- Who We Are and Why We Wrote This Book
- Why Behavior Interventions Are Important
- How Our Interventions Relate to Positive Behavioral Interventions and Supports (PBIS) and Multi-Tiered System of Supports (MTSS)
- What's in This Book—And How to Use It
- Special Features

Your Needs and Wants

I need to know why I have to change the way I deal with behavioral challenges. I want to know why the interventions are important before I use them.

Questions to Think About as You Read the Chapter

- What are your behavioral expectations for your students?
- What are your biggest behavioral challenges in your classroom?
- How effective are PBIS, MTSS, or other behavioral systems in your classroom?

When people refer to classroom management, they are typically describing a system for teaching, managing, and responding to students' behavior. If student behavior is not managed successfully, the learning environment may be so chaotic, unstructured, and ineffective that teachers cannot teach and students cannot learn. The National Council on Teacher Quality's (NCTQ) report on *Training Future Teachers: Classroom Management* (2013) shared that classroom management was "the top problem" identified by teachers. The report's comments on new teachers are particularly striking: Many new teachers are especially "ill-equipped to move beyond behavioral challenges and into the heart of instruction" (NCTQ 2013, p. 2). In other words, of all the issues teachers face, classroom management is at or near the top of the list, and the result is that teachers are having difficulty teaching because of behavioral issues in the classroom.

The challenges teachers face related to classroom management and responses to misbehaviors are complicated by the issue of teacher education and training. Teachers who took a student behavior survey did not feel they were receiving adequate training to implement behavioral management techniques (EAB Executive Briefing, 2023). Whether the training is at the preservice or in-service level, teachers recognize that they need more professional development specific to behavioral issues.

In addition, the behavioral issues facing classroom teachers have changed. A large majority of teachers said in the EAB survey that their students are behind in developing self-regulation and relationship-building skills compared to pre-COVID students. Even more troubling is a report based on teachers' feedback that students are targeting them with "disruptive behavior and that classroom incidents involving physical violence more than doubled since the beginning of the pandemic" (EAB Press Release, 2023). There has been a dramatic increase in disruptive behavior, and the EAB survey reported that districts and campuses often lack clear and consistent behavior management guidelines as well as preparation and support for teachers as they manage disruptive behavior.

The survey also reported a disconnect between teachers' and administrators' beliefs: The teachers' belief is that more students have significant behavioral issues and demonstrate disruptive behaviors, while administrators tend to believe that behavior problems are confined to a small number of students. There is more agreement between administrators and teachers on factors that contribute to disruptive behavior. Commonly cited factors include family trauma, mental health conditions, changes in parenting, an inadequate amount of play or recreation time, and overexposure to electronic devices (EAB District Leadership Forum, 2019; Fad & Campos, 2021).

As we have tried throughout the years to teach, support, and assist teachers, we keep coming back to the fact that without support for behavior management, effective academic instruction suffers. Moreover, even the most positive, prosocial, and preventative behavior management cannot prevent all misbehavior in the classroom. Even highly educated, well-trained, effective teachers will have to respond to specific misbehaviors. While many problems can be prevented, it is not possible to foresee and prevent every disruptive, annoying, interfering, antisocial, defiant, difficult, negative behavior from occurring in classrooms. Our role, then, is to help teachers prevent as many of these misbehaviors as possible, but also provide them with a resource to help them respond effectively when the behaviors do happen—to support their efforts to teach other prosocial, positive behaviors students can learn instead.

This book aims to be that resource. You probably picked it up because you're having problems with misbehaviors in your classroom. You may have one or more students who are driving you crazy. We get it. You're not alone. We had struggles of our own. Based on our experiences and research, we developed a seven-component model that we used to formulate fifty interventions that can help you. The interventions are time-savers that require minimal preparation. You can implement the interventions immediately, one or multiple at a time (depending on the child), throughout the day, across classroom settings, and with diverse groups of students. When used consistently, the strategies can increase student academic engagement and productivity.

Who We Are and Why We Wrote This Book

Before we get into the details of those interventions, let's back up a moment and share more about who we are and how we got to the topic of behavior management. We are former classroom teachers who have taught general and special education populations. Together, we have decades-worth of experience working with children, preservice teachers, and classroom teachers. We have been interested in children's behavior in the classroom for some time. After all, we both have doctorates in behavior disorders. Kathy has written books on research-based strategies for students with special needs. Many of her recommended interventions focus on instructional delivery, student socialization, and academic development. David's books, on the other hand, are aimed at helping teachers better meet the needs of students who are regularly marginalized. His suggested approaches are designed to promote emotionally safe classrooms that advance students' academic outcomes. After writing books separately, we collaborated to write two books for teachers and school counselors on childhood loneliness (Fad & Campos, 2021) and childhood anxiety (Campos & Fad, 2023). Our interests in these two topics came from many conversations we had about children's mental health in schools. Specifically, we noticed an increasing number of students who struggle to focus their attention on instruction and activities, behave according to teachers' expectations, and interact positively with their peers. We found empirical studies that confirm our observations, which you will see cited throughout this book.

Through our research on childhood loneliness and childhood anxiety, we concluded that many children today come to school with a fragile sense of well-being. By that we mean they are exposed to stressful life events such as parental incarceration or food insecurity. Accessible media exposes them to wars, social upheavals, and regular instances of incivility. Social media is pervasive in their lives; youth today are on their devices for many hours a day.

We find that many children today lack the social skills typically used to make and keep friends who could be a source of emotional support. Many also have not learned healthy coping skills to help them process and manage stressful situations. Furthermore, children's well-being is inseparable from their parents' well-being. The American Academy of Pediatrics (AAP) (2022) explains:

> Parents and caregivers and other supportive adults who are expected to be the safe haven for children are, themselves, increasingly struggling to cope and be nurturing and emotionally available to their

> children . . . As a result, infants and young children experience stress both directly and vicariously, and without the maturity to process their experiences, they often adapt by internalizing the impact.

All of this is to say that many children are at school stressed, which negatively affects their behavior in the classroom. Additionally, children with emotional behavioral disorders and anger and aggressive tendencies are included in the general education classroom. Teachers today who need help with behavior management need research-based interventions that positively impact students. Punishing, shouting at, commanding, removing, or publicly shaming students—just penalizing them, in other words—is not a long-term solution. These practices do not teach good behavior. Nor are these practices reasonable to use on children who have gone through or are experiencing recurring stress and maltreatment. Making them suffer for breaking rules and social conventions is sure to compound matters, kickstarting a cycle of misbehavior followed by punishment that leads to misbehavior that follows with punishment and so forth. We wrote this book to help teachers prevent misbehaviors using positive, prosocial, and proactive practices, not penalization. For small classroom tips that help, see figure I.1.

Why Behavior Interventions Are Important

If students misbehave regularly, they don't learn. It's that simple. The impact of problematic behaviors can lead to poor academic performance and dropping out of school (Yoleri, 2013). The welcome news is that teachers can influence student behaviors. Research finds that students have improved learning outcomes when their teachers use a behavior management plan that prevents disruptive behaviors (Ratcliff et al., 2010; Watson et al., 2016).

Over a third of teachers report that students' behavior problems interfere with their teaching, which is understandable considering that their time is reallocated from instruction to attend to misbehaviors (Kirkpatrick et al., 2022). A 2019 EAB study found that 1,400 elementary school teachers reported losing—on average—2.5 hours of their instructional time per week to deal with children's disruptive behaviors (Bronstein et al., 2021). Misbehaviors also negatively impact teachers' mental health, job retention, and perceived school safety (Black & Fernando, 2014; Bronstein et al., 2021; Närhi et al., 2017). Psychologists have found that dealing with behavior problems is a major cause of stress that often leads to teachers leaving the profession (Kirkpatrick et al., 2022; Simpson et al., 2020).

Interventions in the classroom are critical. Good behavior interventions support students' academic and social-emotional learning, which results in increased instructional engagement and on-task behaviors and decreased discipline problems, such as off-task behaviors and disruptions. When teachers spend less time reacting to disruptive behaviors, they can focus attention on developing students' abilities to follow instructions, complete assignments, and process content, which helps students learn (Hamsho & Eckert, 2021).

Interventions also help students develop skills for self-regulation, coping with stress, and maintaining social relationships. Children who regularly misbehave often have impaired social relationships with peers, which keeps them from working collaboratively and developing friendships (McDaniel et al., 2017). Understandably, children do not want to play with, befriend, or work with other students they believe can harm them. Children who have social skills deficits regularly display behavior problems (McDaniel et al., 2017). Young children who have low social competence have increased chances of developing internalizing and externalizing behavior problems (Sheaffer et al., 2021). They need to be taught interpersonal skills, prosocial behaviors (like sharing, helping, cooperating), and self-management strategies.

At the extreme end of interpersonal relationship misbehavior is bullying. Children who bully risk suicidal ideation, violent behavior in adulthood, and long-term psychosomatic problems. Victims of bullies can experience poor academic achievement, internalizing problems, low self-esteem, headaches, sleep difficulties, and suicidal ideation (Bjärehed et al., 2021). By contrast, when students have positive social relationships with their classmates, they have higher academic engagement and achievement (McDaniel et al., 2017).

Overlooking misbehavior and discipline problems is never a good solution. It often leads to serious consequences. Without behavior intervention, children can continue to be difficult, defiant, and disruptive as they progress through school, and in many cases, their behaviors become more problematic (McDaniel et al., 2017). Behavior problems often increase with age, resulting in greater likelihood for developing antisocial behavior, substance abuse, and delinquency (Bjärehed et al., 2021). All this puts students at risk for further unfavorable outcomes, which include developing mental health conditions and dropping out of school (Hamsho & Eckert, 2021).

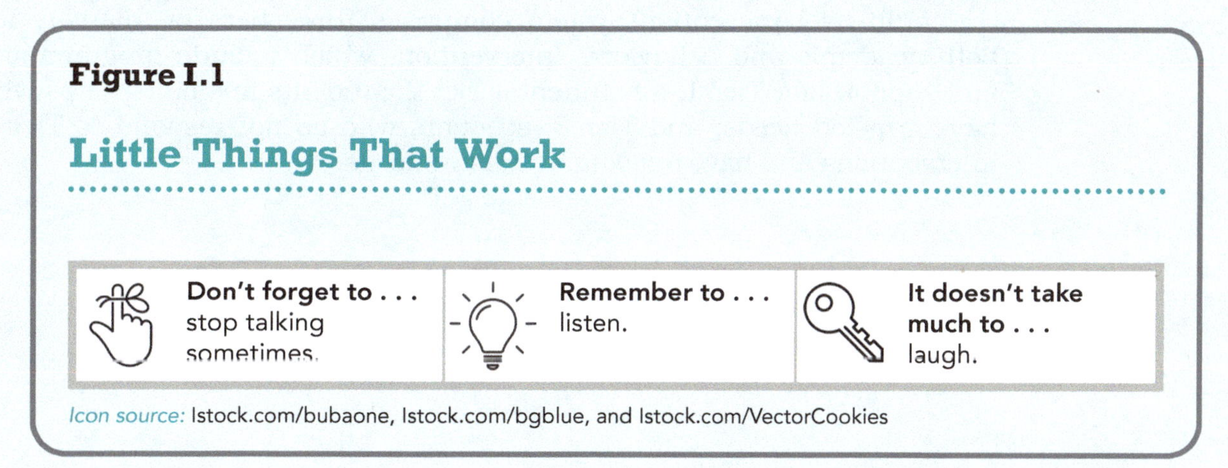

How Our Interventions Relate to PBIS and MTSS

In the area of behavior management, two comprehensive programs that emphasize positive approaches to teaching and maintaining prosocial, positive behaviors are used in schools nationwide. Because our recommended preventative practices (chapters 2, 3, and 4) and our fifty interventions are also positive, proactive, and prosocial, we want to explain the two programs and how our model can be used in tandem with them.

PBIS

One of the most promising educational initiatives of the past several years is the development and dissemination of the Positive Behavioral Interventions and Supports system, known widely as PBIS. PBIS is being used nationwide for several reasons, all of which work toward the big-picture goal of supporting positive behaviors on campuses. Banks and Obiakor (2015) summarized the characteristics of PBIS: (a) using data-based decision-making related to behavior, (b) developing a set of behavior expectations, both schoolwide and classroom related, (c) teaching common behavioral expectations, and (d) acknowledging positive, appropriate behaviors. These common characteristics are based on positive actions and positive goals related to improving student behavior on campuses. In addition, they and many other authors recognize two other goals of PBIS: decreasing inappropriate behaviors and reducing office discipline referrals, primarily through prevention.

MTSS

Another recent initiative related to positive behaviors in schools is the MTSS model (Multi-Tiered Systems of Support), often referred to as tiered interventions. MTSS is a framework designed to support students' social, emotional, and behavioral needs. It has four key components: screening, multi-level prevention, progress monitoring, and data-based decision-making. According to the Center of Multi-Tiered System of Supports (2024), the multi-level prevention system comprises three tiers of intensity for both academic and behavioral intervention, which include programming and supports for Tier 1, all students; Tier 2, students in small groups who have targeted needs; and Tier 3, students who do not respond to Tier 2 interventions and have ongoing, intensive needs.

At Tier 1, interventions are designed to teach and model appropriate behavior and agreed-upon supports aligned to students' needs. A positive school climate and consistent supports are essential. At Tier 2, educators implement agreed-upon interventions for students who need additional support. The interventions should be supported by research and regularly evaluated for effectiveness. Tier 3 interventions provide support to those students who need more intensive, specialized supports. At this level, those students with persistent, chronic behavioral issues should be provided with individualized interventions and data should be reviewed on their efficacy.

OUR INTERVENTIONS

When teachers think of these systems of intervention as separate entities, it can be overwhelming. In our experience, teachers often get bogged down or overwhelmed by the system and its monitoring component. They often lose sight of the daily basics: what they can and should do to teach positive, prosocial behaviors and prevent misbehavior. Our priority in helping teachers with behavioral issues is to provide well researched, practical ideas for prevention. However, we recognize that not all misbehavior can be prevented. That's why we developed interventions for the most common misbehaviors that disrupt teaching and learning in the classroom. These interventions are also based on the principles of PBIS and can be used in elementary classrooms at Tiers 1, 2, and 3 of intervention.

HOW WE DESIGNED THE INTERVENTIONS

This book provides you with the tools to build relationships with students, manage their behaviors, and help them develop appropriate social-emotional skills. We identified the behavioral problems that teachers struggle with the most, then created practical and easy-to-use interventions based on what researchers find is most effective when dealing with those behaviors. We wanted interventions to teach—not correct—behaviors, which, if used with fidelity, would develop students' academic, social-emotional, and behavioral skills. From our research, we found that teachers' instruction is most disrupted by students who demonstrate the behaviors found in the figure I.2.

Figure I.2

Top Ten Student Behaviors That Disrupt Instruction

1. Talking out	The student talks without permission, sometimes interrupting, bothering others, and making inappropriate comments.
2. Moving around	The student leaves their seat or work area without permission.
3. Arriving late/delaying start of classwork	The student is often tardy to school or slow to begin to work.
4. Failing to cooperate with others	The student has difficulties working with others, cooperating in groups, and getting along.
5. Failing to complete assignments/avoiding work/often unorganized	The student fails to complete assignments, especially independent work.
6. Refusing to follow directions	The student refuses to follow classroom rules and procedures, including teacher directions, and may argue when given directions.
7. Avoiding social interactions/isolating themselves	The student avoids interactions with others and does not ask to join activities or try to include others.
8. Failing to cope with typical classroom expectations because of worries and perfectionism	The student has difficulty coping and expresses worries and fear of failure; they may procrastinate or stop trying.
9. Tantrumming to get their way	The student tantrums, cries, or yells when they don't get their way.
10. Violating classroom norms to the point of negatively impacting others	The student escalates their behavior to uncivil and/or threatening behavior.

With these behaviors in mind, we created our fifty interventions using a model that consists of seven research-based components that use positive, proactive, and prosocial practices. The components are also based on our experiences and discussions with teachers, specialists, and school leadership teams over the fundamental elements of effective behavior intervention. Teachers can use these seven essential components as starting points when considering solutions for other challenging behaviors, too. Any behavior intervention, for that matter, can be written and implemented using one or more of the seven components. See the components and their descriptions in the figure I.3.

Figure I.3

Seven Essential Components of Behavior Intervention

	COMPONENT	WHAT WE MEAN
	Use your attention and relationship	• Be mentally present with students. • Be physically nearby and focused on them (proximity matters!). • Meet their wellness needs. • Commit to strengthening bonds with them. • Balance instruction with appreciating their personality traits.
	Signal, warn, restate expectations	• Use cues as reminders. • Use visuals or auditory signals. • Remind students of expectations and consequences.
	Teach and reteach	• Teach prosocial behaviors that students have not learned. • Teach positive behaviors instead of expecting them. • Reteach prosocial behaviors that students do not use consistently.
	Be flexible: change activities, resources, or delivery	• Vary instruction to keep students motivated. • Use student interests and learning styles in activities. • Maintain consistent routines and procedures but adapt teaching methods to give students something to look forward to.
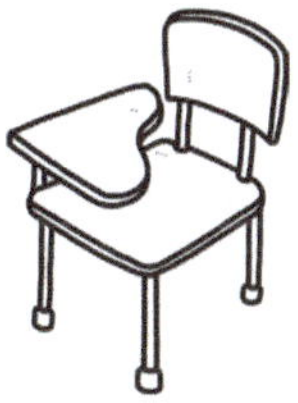	Change the environment	• Rearrange the classroom to meet the needs of individuals and groups of students. • Address movement, seating, materials, etc.
	Use positive reinforcement	• Use a consequence system with rewards for prosocial behaviors and/or meeting goals. • Respond to positive, prosocial behaviors with descriptive praise. • Have charts and menus that list privileges that students can earn.
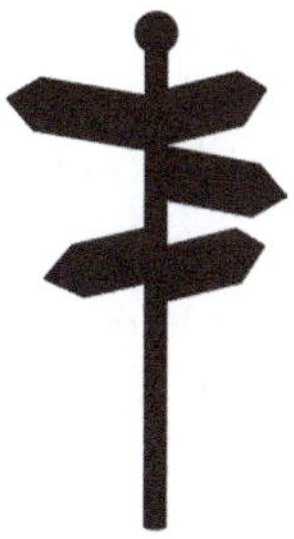	Provide choices; respect individuality	• Give students choices and options. • Let students decide when and how to use their earned consequences. • Allow students choices about movement, seating, assignments, etc.

Icon source: Istock.com/Turac Novruzova; Istock.com/Iuliia Konovaliuk; Istock.com/Turac Novruzova; Istock.com/ourlifelooklike-balloon; Istock.com/owattaphotos; Istock.com/Sudowoodo; and Istock.com/Artem Stepanov

As an example of how the components of our model are incorporated into an intervention, see the image below of Study Buddies (Intervention 22, in Part IV, found on p. 139).

INTERVENTION 22: STUDY BUDDIES

Misbehavior: Failure to Complete Assignments

Essential Components of Behavior Intervention Addressed

- Teach/reteach
- Be flexible
- Use positive reinforcement
- Provide choices

Need:

- *Study Buddies* Cards

Know:

Students often do not complete assignments because they can't remember the assignment, can't find their materials, or are just so unorganized it is difficult for them to do their work. They often need help with organization, but busy teachers do not always have the time to help them. Teaching students to help each other is a great way to provide support while continuing instruction in the classroom.

Do:

1. Each week assign students to pairs as study buddies. Do this thoughtfully and vary your assignments.
2. Copy and laminate the *Study Buddies* Cards (figure 7.26) so that each student has one.
3. Before the start of the day or lesson, give each student a *Study Buddies* Card.
4. Ask students to put their name and their buddy's name on the card. Set the timer for three minutes (give or take, depending on your students' ages) and have them check supplies and homework. Be clear about what supplies are needed and what the homework was. Put a tally mark on the tally sheet next to each Buddy pair that does their check.
5. In the afternoon, ask students to do a *Study Buddies* check of homework assignments and books/papers that need to go home. Again, give them a tally mark for completion.
6. At the end of the week, provide incentives for study buddies who completed their cards each day and helped keep each other on track.

We also kept some important criteria in mind when designing the fifty interventions Each of them meet those criteria, descriptions of which follow.

Positive. Negative, punitive approaches do not change behavior. Teaching positive new skills is a lot more productive than eliminating negative ones. (Not to mention that spending a school day in a negative frame of mind is tiring and demoralizing.)

Prosocial. Teachers have to promote positive social behaviors. They have to *teach* behavior, in other words, not just manage or control it. Many students come to school lacking basic social skills that teachers expect them to know. But if the students have not been taught those skills elsewhere, then it is left to schools to teach them. Knowing how to join or leave a group, how to share an idea, and how to give a compliment are basic skills that will be new learning for some students.

Research based. Some interventions might be cool and cute and fun, but if there is no research to support their use, they can be a waste of time. If there is no good reason to expect success, it is better not to use an intervention at all.

Practical. Classrooms are busy places and teachers need access to interventions that are easy to understand, simple to implement, quick to apply, and get results. Interventions should not require complicated lesson plans or long, drawn-out explanations. Instead, they should include ready-to-use forms, tools, and visual examples.

Varied and individualized. Not all students respond to the same interventions in the same way. Even when students do respond to an intervention, their behavior change may not last. So, teachers need a varied and expansive menu of strategies that they can use with a diverse class of students. Not everything works or works the first time. Teachers need options so that when they need to try something new, it is an easy transition to another available intervention.

Respectful and sensitive. Teachers increasingly recognize the impact of social stressors and recurring maltreatment on some students. Mental health issues are a serious and increasingly critical issue for modern-day students. Behavior interventions must be thoughtful, considerate, sensitive, and respectful, while still maintaining high expectations for students.

Culturally and socially accepting. No judgment or suppositions should be included in the interventions' explanations, directions, examples, or reproducible forms. Interventions should demonstrate a lack of bias in all discussions and suggestions. Because some students have a history in school that has not been positive, interventions should start with the relationship between the teacher and the student.

Enjoyable. Interventions that include humor, games, and interactive options encourage teachers to be consistent in using them. If activities are enjoyable, they are more likely to be used often enough to make a difference.

What's in This Book—And How to Use It

While we know that you likely need help with the behavioral challenges in your classroom, it is hard to gauge the kind of reader you are. So we're going to differentiate our instruction here, and ask you to choose the best place for you to start based on your needs. Keep in mind that this book is divided into four parts:

- Part I is an introduction and describes our rationale for how to think about children's behavior and misbehavior.
- Part II is about preventing misbehaviors and presents good practices for creating a positive learning environment.
- Part III discusses our model and supporting research.
- Part IV presents our fifty interventions.

PART I: INTRODUCTION AND RATIONALE

Chapter 1 discusses our definitions of behavior and misbehavior and asks you to reflect on your own definitions and expectations. We consider some reasons why children misbehave in the classroom and discuss classroom culture and individualism. You'll learn some ways to help students feel included, valued, and comfortable in your classroom. Chapter 2 explains what we mean by "positive, proactive, and prosocial practices." You'll learn how to make your behavior management radiate positivity.

PART II: PREVENTING MISBEHAVIORS

Chapter 3 offers recommendations for setting up your behavior management system. You'll learn how to establish rules, use consequences, communicate, and be assertive, consistent, and respectful. Chapter 4 discusses skills that help students prevent misbehavior, including academic skills, self-regulation skills, and calming skills. You'll learn some ideas for teaching, modeling, and practicing those techniques with students.

PART III: INTERVENTION

Chapter 5 goes into more depth about our seven-component model, first outlined in the figure on page 11 (and again in figure 5.1). You'll learn why you should follow our model. Chapter 6 goes into more depth about the top ten misbehaviors we selected. You'll learn how we came up with that list and why other behaviors aren't on it.

PART IV: FIFTY INTERVENTIONS FOR THE TOP TEN MISBEHAVIORS

This section includes instructions for using the interventions, a matrix to help you choose which intervention to use based on what it addresses, and the details of all fifty interventions. The interventions address the most common misbehaviors in the classroom. The interventions are positive, proactive, and prosocial because each incorporates one or more essential components for behavior management. With no time-consuming lesson plans to write or forms to create, the reproducible pages that accompany the interventions are immediately useable and include forms, charts, tickets, prompts, reminder cards, and much more. The prevention and intervention recommendations contained here make for a valuable toolbox for any teacher.

Special Features

In each chapter, we provide special features that offer reading guidance and helpful behavior management tips. These will help you relate the content to your own experience, consider even more positive actions you can take, and reflect on your growth:

- The box at the beginning of each chapter includes brief notes about what content you'll find there and what needs the chapter addresses, along with some questions to keep in mind as you read.
- **Little Things That Work** boxes offer quick reminders to take care of yourself, your attitude, and your approaches.
- **Classroom Connections** boxes present practical ideas to use in the classroom.
- **Pow! How? Now!** boxes appear at the end of each chapter. Rather than provide you with a summary of what you just read, we would like you to think about what you have read, how it changes what you think and do, and what steps you will take next.

CLASSROOM CONNECTION

Teachers should help children face problems of everyday life, especially at school. To help students commit to tasks rather than pout, waste time, or disrupt others when they feel overwhelmed, one teacher writes on the board what they can do:

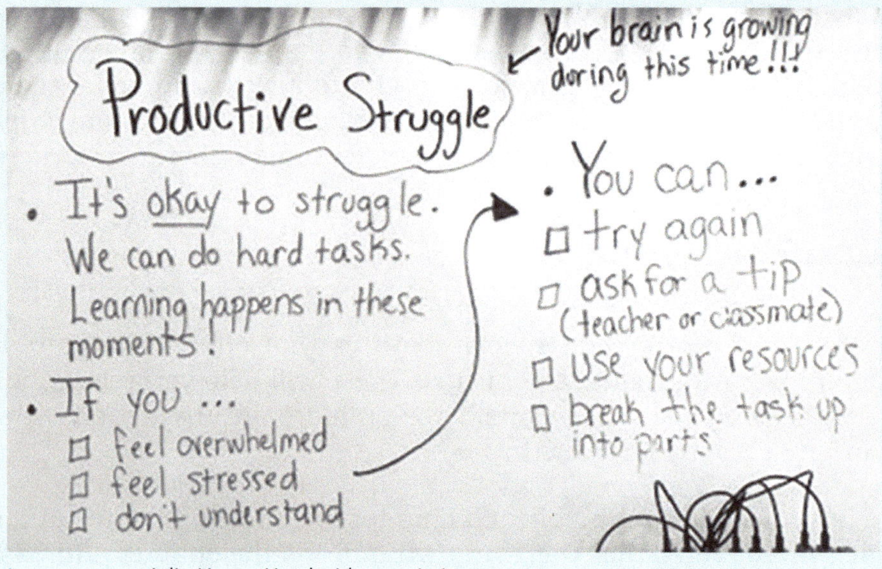

Image source: Julie Howe. Used with permission.

Pow! How? Now!	
	What are your reactions to what you read so far?
	How will you use this information?
	What does this mean, especially with your most challenging students?

Icon source: Istock.com/nazarkru and Istock.com/lineartestpilot

DEFINITION AND CAUSES OF MISBEHAVIOR

CHAPTER 1

What's in This Chapter

- Teacher Needs
- *Behavior* and *Misbehavior* Defined
- Classroom Culture and Individual Differences
- Factors That Lead to Misbehavior

Your Needs and Wants

I need to know more about what is meant by the term *misbehavior*, and I need to understand some reasons why children misbehave in the classroom. I want to know some ways to help students feel included, valued, and comfortable in my classroom.

Questions to Think About as You Read the Chapter

- What professional development on behavior management has been most effective for you?
- How does your school or district define misbehavior? Do you agree with that definition?
- What are some reasons your students misbehave?

This chapter addresses teachers' need for a plan that helps them with managing student behavior. It defines *behavior* and *misbehavior* as they are used in this book. And it wraps up with a discussion on cultural and individual differences and on factors that lead some children to misbehave, so you can understand why it's important to use behavioral approaches that do not insult or demoralize children.

Teacher Needs

A behavior management plan that increases academically engaged behaviors and decreases behavior problems is essential for teachers. Without one, a larger pool of children will be off task, disengaged, and disruptive. Teachers who use techniques and interventions to cultivate calm, productive, active, and engaging learning environments also help children develop social emotional skills. Research finds that teachers who effectively manage challenging behaviors positively impact students' emotional stability (Brokamp et al., 2019) and sense of self-efficacy (Floress & Beschta, 2018).

But even though teachers recognize that behavior management is the hardest part of teaching, it is *the* area in which they receive the least training (Hirsch et al. 2019), and they lack the resources and support to adequately address misbehaviors (Hoffman & Kuvalanka, 2019). A survey of one thousand three hundred public school teachers revealed that nearly half mentioned their need for information and training on how to support student well-being and did not have enough control over classroom management strategies (Charles Butt Foundation, 2022). Another study found that less than half of teachers reported participating in professional development focused on managing student behaviors, and of those who did, only 62 percent considered it useful (Hirsch et al., 2019). New teachers do not fare any better in behavior management. They also report not having knowledge, preparation, and mastery of prevention and intervention strategies (Simpson et al. 2020), which contributes to their feeling anxious, helpless, and incapable of affecting student behavior (Hirsch et al., 2019).

This need for training, resources, and support may contribute to teachers inadvertently cultivating environments that invite misbehavior, especially when teachers overreact to inappropriate conduct, seem uncaring, or use management strategies inadequately or inconsistently (Bronstein et al., 2021; Hoffman & Kuvalanka, 2019).

Behavior and *Misbehavior* Defined

Before we move further, let's talk about what we mean by *behavior* and *misbehavior*. There is an obvious definition of behavior—the way someone behaves. However, that definition does not provide a clear, complete description of student behavior in classrooms. For the purposes of this book, we use the IRIS Center (2012) definition of behavior specific to education:

> *Behavior* is something that a person does that can be observed, measured, and repeated. When we clearly define behavior, we specifically describe actions (e.g., Sam talks during class instruction). We do not refer to personal motivation, internal processes, or feelings (e.g., Sam talks during class instruction to get attention). (p. 3)

When behavior is defined as an action a student takes, teachers can describe it and collect and summarize data about it. They can ask and answer questions about it: How often does it occur? Is it increasing or decreasing? When does it occur? What does it look and sound like? Moreover, clearly defining a behavior allows teachers to determine the environmental conditions when it occurs (e.g., Does it only happen at one time of day? With a specific person? In one subject area?). When teachers have information on a student behavior, they can contemplate the purpose of the behavior, the motivation for the behavior, the feelings behind the behavior, the student's history and personal characteristics, demographic information, student records, and so on. In other words, they can hypothesize about the behavior based on what they observe and learn. Then, they can decide what to do next.

The definition of school or classroom *misbehavior* is not nearly as clear cut. *Misconduct, discipline problems*, and *disruptive behaviors* are labels found throughout the research literature that have various definitions (Sun & Shek, 2012). This is problematic. If teachers and administrators do not agree on which behaviors are misbehaviors, how can they design an equitable and consistent system of expectations and range of responses to misbehavior? Because different cultures and ethnic groups have specific expectations for behavior, how do teachers agree on what constitutes misbehavior? While there are requirements and protections for students with disabilities related to misbehaviors, are these always clearly understood and implemented? Dealing with misbehavior is complicated.

For our purposes, we describe *misbehaviors* as those that interfere with or disrupt teaching and learning, are likely to have a negative impact on students' or teachers' well-being, interfere with healthy social relationships, and/or damage the positive climate of the classroom. We also believe that misbehaviors in daily doses can be demoralizing, exhausting, and discouraging to teachers—not to mention that students who regularly misbehave risk peer alienation and loss of trust and belief in teachers and the value of education. As figure 1.1 shows, even small efforts to reach out can be useful classroom management tools.

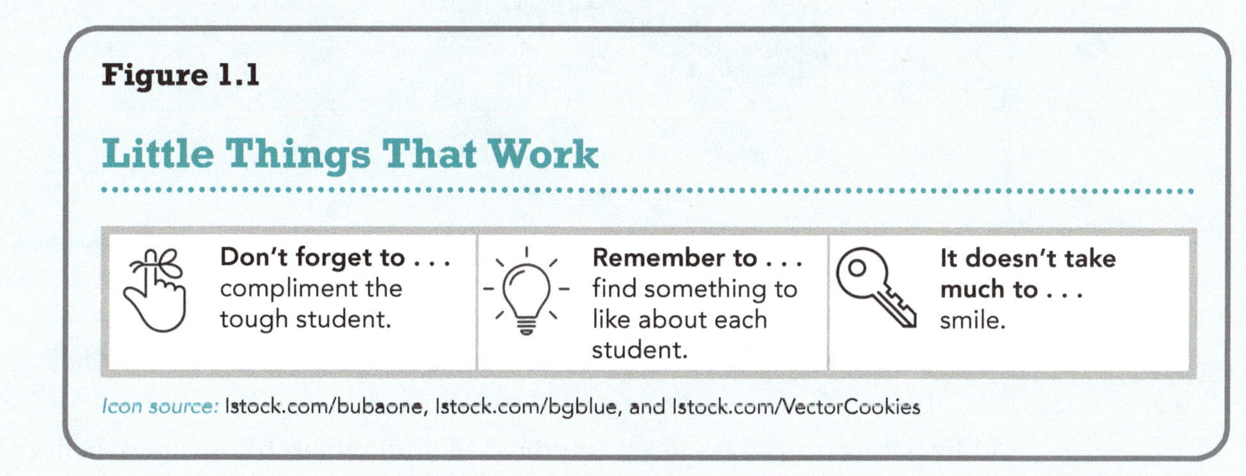

CLASSROOM CONNECTION

Model and practice your behavioral expectations regularly so that all students understand them. Students can role-play the expectations and alternate with a contrasting portrayal. They can also role-play a variety of social skills. Role-playing has been shown to be an effective method of teaching children from diverse backgrounds. Edwards writes that role-playing helps students "become more attentive to the various voices in the classroom and to recognize differences and similarities among them" (Edwards, 2004, p.341). Using headbands is one way to get students to assume roles to play. For example, if you are teaching students to listen to each other, you could give a "talker" headband to one student and a "listener" headband to another. Then, have them role-play listening (e.g., the talker looks at the partner, stands nearby but not too close, uses a conversation noise level, etc. while the other looks at the talker, stands closely, nods, and so forth). After a few minutes of practice, have them switch roles. Headbands could also be used to role play asking for and giving help, sharing (e.g., how to politely borrow someone else's supplies, how to grant permission for supply use, how to use someone else's supplies with care, etc.), and including others in activities (e.g., how to invite others to join lesson discussions, social conversations, and outdoor play).

Image source: Istock.com/kali9

Classroom Culture and Individual Differences

Addressing cultural issues and individual differences in the classroom can make some teachers nervous. They might worry about saying or doing the wrong thing or maybe stress over not doing enough. But this discussion does not have to be frightening or overwhelming. Taking a commonsense, positive approach can make a big difference in the classroom without compromising anyone's beliefs or sense of safety and well-being. Weinstein et al. (2003) suggest that we recognize some basics related to culture. They write, "First, we must recognize that we are all cultural beings, with our own beliefs, biases, and assumptions about human behavior," and "second, we must acknowledge the cultural, racial, ethnic, and class differences that exist among people" (p. 270). The good news is that everyone can acquire cultural knowledge. Some steps to acquire this knowledge are simple and others are more complicated, but teachers can start by being willing to learn. Knowledge about your students' backgrounds and experiences and their cultural expectations related to relationships and discipline can help you develop successful classroom management expectations. You can build a style of interaction that is comfortable for both you and students. For example, students who are recent immigrants and have been exposed to violence need calm learning environments. They need teachers who manage the classroom with predictability (i.e., teachers who administer routines, rules, and procedures consistently and fairly), interact with students patiently with a smile (no sudden surprises or loud overreactions), and protect them from what could be embarrassing or troubling situations.

All students should feel like they belong and should know that they are in an environment that will help them succeed. This concept of inclusiveness has been a focus of special and general education teaching teams for many years, as they have worked toward the successful inclusion of students with disabilities into general education environments. Because school success is not just about academics, positive social experiences, including relationships with others and behaviors that facilitate learning, are critical. The value of inclusion is consistently recognized and appreciated by the school community, especially parents and families. Educators, of course, realize that schools and classrooms in the US are often very diverse and include not just students with disabilities, but also students whose linguistic, cultural, racial, economic, and ethnic characteristics may vary from many of their classmates and/or from their teachers.

Long et al. (2019) point out some related demographic information that impacts student behavior and classroom management, including these facts:

1. Many public schools serve a majority of students whose eligibility for free and reduced lunch indicates their economic disadvantage, which can impact their background, experiences, and behavior.
2. Despite an increase in the number of students with diverse backgrounds, the majority of the teaching force is still overwhelmingly female, White, monolingual, and economically middle class. This contradiction is not problematic in and of itself, but it has the potential to challenge both teachers' and students' understanding of each other's norms and expectations.
3. Long et al. (2019) go on to point out this statistic: According to US public school data, some schools with a majority of low income and ethnically or racially minority students often rely on exclusionary discipline practices. Because office discipline referrals historically

overrepresent students with disabilities and Black students, infusing strategies that consider students' cultural, linguistic, economic, gender, and disability-related characteristics into PBIS systems and tiered interventions can have a positive impact, reducing referral rates.

Following are a few important steps teachers can take to ensure that *all* students feel included, valued, and comfortable in their classrooms.

Build and maintain authentic relationships with students' families. This is especially important for those students whose families may not feel connected to the education system or the community. This process involves not just communication when problems arise but also positive outreach to get to know them *before* problems arise. For example, call, write, or visit the parents or guardians of each student in your class and, if possible, begin doing so as soon as school starts. Make the contact brief but positive. During planning period or whenever you have a quick break, make calls or write postcards to be mailed, send home a compliment with your school contact information in students' backpacks, or walk out to the pickup line or corner bus stop and meet the parents there. Set a goal of making contact with each family by the end of the first two weeks of school.

Have high expectations for all students. Teachers should communicate clear and consistent behavioral expectations for all students. These expectations should be reasonable, and students who need additional support and instruction should be provided with both. As we discussed in the definitions of behavior and misbehavior, it is important that teachers and administrators agree on what constitutes misbehavior and expectations that are reasonable. School-wide and district-wide behavior systems like PBIS (Positive Behavioral Interventions and Supports) and MTSS (Multi-Tiered System of Supports), which we described in the introduction, rely on educators' agreement on positive behavior standards, what behaviors constitute misbehaviors, reasonable school-wide and classroom expectations, and consistent responses to both expectations and misbehaviors. While teachers certainly have their own expectations and input into group norms, it is not acceptable for teachers to disregard the economic, social, cultural, linguistic, and disability characteristics of the communities they serve. Reasonableness and consistency are important so that all students feel safe and secure in the knowledge that while they are expected to meet standards of behavior, they will be treated fairly and with kindness and acceptance.

The keys to this strategy are simplicity and clarity. Several times in this book, we suggest the use of a looks like/sounds like chart to show students exactly what is expected of them. Teachers can take this one step further by adding a third column to the chart: "How can I help you?" Telling a student that you will support them as they learn a new behavior will be helpful to both of you. The student will likely feel more comfortable asking for help when they do not understand rather than moving forward aimlessly. Figure 1.2 is an example of a chart that shows behavior expectations for group work.

Figure 1.2

Group Work

Looks Like 	Sounds Like 	How can I help you? 
Taking turns Sharing materials Staying with your group	One person talking at a time Giving each other feedback Asking questions	Repeat the directions and write them on the board Help me start I need a buddy to check my work I need someone to tell me how much time I have left

Icon source: Istock.com/checha, Istock.com/Hiranmay Baidya and Istock.com/cnythzl

Listen respectfully. Listening is key for teachers. While it is sometimes difficult to listen when there is so much commotion in the classroom, it is important that students feel heard. Whether through speech or body language, teachers should convey that they are reasonable and that they care about all of their students. One strategy is to use one of these phrases in response to student questions: "Great question. I have time to answer that right now," or "Great question. I can't answer that right now, but here's a question cone. I'll be back to answer when I have a moment." Use a mini cone, a plastic cup, or a cardboard cube (each with a question mark on it) as the signal. Do your best to return with an answer within a few minutes.

Follow through. Teachers need to do what they say they will do in order for students to trust them. Consistency helps students know what to expect. Chapter 2 discusses establishing expectations and following through with consequences, which help students see why and how everyone will be treated fairly and consistently. Posting a problem/solution chart and using it as a teaching tool is an excellent way to ensure consistent follow-through. See the example below for a chart that addresses some common classroom misbehaviors. Have a discussion with the students to come up with student solutions before explaining what the teacher solutions (consequences) will be if their solutions don't work. The disruptive behaviors are written in the "problems" column, and the consequences are listed in the "solutions" column. After documenting and discussing the behavioral issues you've seen with students and how you will address them (with student input), explain that the solutions need to be fair and consistently followed. Figure 1.3 can serve as a reminder to everyone what will happen under what circumstances.

Figure 1.3

Problems and Solutions

PROBLEMS	STUDENT SOLUTIONS	TEACHER SOLUTIONS
A student is keeping others from learning by making loud noises.	We can ask the student to please be quiet. We can ask the student if they need help. We can signal the student with a "sh" sign.	I can put a quiet sign on the student's desk to remind them to be quiet. I can stand near the student. I can ask the student to move to the quiet area to work.
A student is saying mean things to others.	We can ask the student to stop saying mean things. We can move away from the student. If the student keeps saying mean things, we can tell the teacher.	I can talk to the student in the hallway and remind them about the expectation to be kind to others. I can ask the student to write an apology note to the classmate they were mean to. If the student keeps being mean, I can call their parent or guardian and explain how they have been treating their classmates.

Be a team player. While it may seem like this suggestion, which refers to your interactions with colleagues, doesn't impact students, it likely does in several important ways. Consulting with other teachers, specialists, and the school leadership team provides insight and knowledge, especially about students with special needs, students experiencing stressful family or community situations, and students who may not have other positive connections in their lives. Talk to parents, caregivers, and prior teachers of students who are struggling; they often have valuable knowledge that can be used to support the student. In turn, you can share what you've learned about the student with their future teachers or specialists.

Factors That Lead to Misbehavior

It has been reported that teachers have agonized over behavior problems in mainstream classrooms for a long time (Busacca et al., 2015), but a recent survey found that teachers believe that behavior problems in classrooms have been increasing steadily for the last few years (Hoffman & Kuvalanka, 2019). Teachers can expect challenging behaviors to be present in one out of five children (Stichter et al., 2009), which is problematic given that misbehaviors significantly affect *all* students in the classroom. The reality is that there are many reasons that behavior problems present themselves in the classroom. Knowing factors that lead to misbehavior can help teachers design interventions that meet individual student needs. Here are some:

The student has a disability. There is a strong likelihood that the student's disability will affect their behavior during instruction, especially if they have an emotional behavioral disorder, autism spectrum disorder, or ADHD. By definition of those disabilities, children will likely have behavior and social skills challenges. Up to 80 percent of students with disabilities demonstrate problem behaviors (Kirkpatrick et al., 2022).

The student has undiagnosed mental health issues. Some children misbehave because they have undiagnosed mental health issues. They are not yet identified as having an emotional behavioral disorder (such as oppositional defiant disorder, conduct disorder, or mood and anxiety disorders), but their behaviors nonetheless present as criteria for such a diagnosis. So, they have serious behavior problems at school, which includes having difficulty with social relationships. They may not show empathy or respect for peers; they may be pessimistic; they may react poorly to stress (e.g., they tantrum when they do not get their way), and so on. These behaviors contrast with indicators of good mental health, like effectively using self-regulation and coping skills, showing positivity, and building social relationships (Centers for Disease Control and Prevention [CDC], 2022). The CDC emphasizes that poor mental health and patterns of symptoms can develop into mental disorders.

The student has difficulty adjusting to school. Children may have difficulty adjusting to school and the classroom for a number of reasons (Yoleri, 2013). They may not want to, or know how to, or find it difficult to conform to rules and routines and therefore avoid teachers' expectations for attention, task completion, and emotion regulation. Some students may not enjoy their physical environment, classmates, or teacher and act out their disapproval.

Students believe they are not respected. Behavior problems may emerge when children feel that teachers do not respect them as valued members of the learning community or do not give them deserved attention, honor, consideration, concern, appreciation, care, and admiration (Caldalerra et al., 2021; Tomlinson, 2011). Expect behavior problems when classroom management practices do not correspond to the needs of the students. For example, a first grader may have continuous outbursts because he feels shame when his teacher moves his card or clip to a color that represents misbehavior and is on public display for the day. Fifth graders may protest with misbehavior when the teacher punishes the whole class because of the actions of one student.

The instruction is too teacher focused. Children will disrupt instruction when lessons and activities are teacher centered, use too many worksheets, and follow dreary routines. Teachers are likely to witness misbehavior when they teach without empathy and enforce no-talking rules throughout the day; keep students seated in rows; and use topics, materials, and books that bore children. One study found that students were better behaved and most engaged when their teachers implemented interactive lessons and collaborative group activities than when they were coerced to focus all their attention on the teacher and had individual seatwork to complete (Zoromski et al. 2021). Evidence suggests that the format of student work (i.e., independent, paired/partner, or small group) is strongly associated with engagement rates.

Parenting style affects the child's behavior. Parenting styles (i.e., how parents discipline their children) also have a big impact on children's behavior. A large body of research finds that parents who are very harsh or very permissive are more likely to have children who are aggressive and anxious than parents who are not (Dempster et al., 2012; Mak et al., 2020; Vučković et al., 2021). Psychologists have found that parents who are authoritative and punitive, discipline inconsistently, or lack warmth or positive involvement tend to have children with behavioral problems (Loona & Kamal, 2012). It also seems that parents who have high degrees of stress levels tend to have negative parenting styles, which often leads to internalizing and externalizing behavioral problems (Mak et al.). As a side note, internalizing behaviors are those that are focused inwards (like when children are depressed or have excessive worry), and externalizing behaviors are presented outward, such as when children are defiant, hostile, or physically aggressive.

Problems in the student's community affect their behavior. Community violence (i.e., witnessing violence in the community, being a victim of such violence, or being subject to both) can negatively impact children's behavior (Kersten et al., 2017). Research finds that children who are regularly exposed to violence in their community are more likely to report behavioral and psychological problems (internalizing, externalizing, and PTSD symptoms) than children who are not (Al'Uqdah et al., 2015; Mohammed et al., 2015). So, some children's misbehavior in the classroom may be attributed to what they witness in the streets, the neighborhood, and other public spaces (Darawshy et al., 2020).

Pow! How? Now!	
	What are your reactions to what you read so far?
	How will you use this information that you just read?
	What does this information mean, especially with your most challenging students?

Icon source: Istock.com/nazarkru and Istock.com/lineartestpilot

CHAPTER 2

POSITIVE, PROACTIVE, AND PROSOCIAL PRACTICES

What's in This Chapter

- Positive Behavior Management Practices
- Building Relationships Is Important
- Proactive Behavior Management Practices
- Prosocial Behavior Management Practices

Your Needs and Wants

I need to know more about being positive, proactive, and prosocial. I want to know ways my behavior management can radiate positivity.

Questions to Think About as You Read the Chapter

- What are your initial reactions to when your students misbehave?
- How do you prevent or keep misbehaviors from escalating?
- What behavioral skills have you taught your students?

In the last chapter, you learned about teacher needs and explored factors that explain why some children misbehave in the classroom. We explained that behavior management systems should emphasize positivity rather than punitive or disciplinary undertones. The introduction stressed how popular models of intervention, namely PBIS and MTSS, use positive approaches to teach and maintain prosocial, positive behaviors. The seven essential components of our model use similar approaches to support students academically, behaviorally, socially, and emotionally. But what exactly are positive, proactive, and prosocial practices for managing students' behaviors?

When considering solutions for challenging behaviors, we strongly recommend positive, proactive, and prosocial intervention. It may offer some immediate relief to use punitive, disciplinary measures to address misbehavior, but such measures are typically ineffectual. Psychologists and education experts find that teachers who penalize students often report feeling incompetent and emotionally exhausted when they do (Coy & Kostewicz, 2018). These teachers witness increased aggression, vandalism, truancy, and tardiness (Caldalerra et al., 2021; Ruef et al., 1998). Additionally, intervention that removes students from the learning environment to restrictive settings compromises academic achievement and rates of school completion (Fallon et al. 2020). Referrals to the office, suspensions, and expulsions should be used as a last resort and only when students risk harming themselves or others.

These are some examples of dealing negatively with challenging behaviors:

- Losing control (e.g., screaming at children)
- Reacting angrily as behaviors occur by yelling commands, such as *Stop that!*, *Sit down!*, *Be quiet!*, and *Now!*, or by shushing students or snapping your fingers at them
- Only punishing students by taking away recess, a festivity, or free time, or by forcing students to write lines (e.g., forcing students to copy a sentence repeatedly, such as *I will stay in my seat when I'm told to*)
- Using threatening statements (such as "If you do that one more time, I'm kicking you out of this classroom" or "I'm not going to tell you this again")
- Insulting students with sarcastic remarks, such as "I guess you need to be told multiple times" or "It's really hard to like you"
- Isolating students by seating them away from classmates or sending them to time-out or to another classroom
- Referring students to the office or in school suspension, which results in lost learning opportunities
- Singling out students' behavioral shortcomings on a chart (We'll address this again later; some of the strategies in Part IV may seem like making a public declaration of a student's behavioral status, but they are designed to help develop a specific skill)

Traditional perspectives on behavior management tend to have negative undertones (Ruef et al., 1998). Teachers who have a traditional attitude on misbehaviors tend to view the child as the problem. Some teachers think that because the student does not behave like the other children, something is wrong with them. In addition to dealing negatively with behaviors (as in the list above), they may rely on others (i.e., principals, school specialists) to take care of the student's misbehavior. This may reduce their own authority/effectiveness.

Positive Behavior Management Practices

Adopting a positive approach toward managing children's behavior, on the other hand, means revising whatever negative narrative teachers might have about their challenging students (Lassiter & Campbell, 2019). It means choosing to be empathetic and understanding, and it means working toward increasing appropriate behaviors (Allday, 2018). With a more positive approach, when teachers witness challenging behavior, their first instinct is to identify the desired behavior they expect to teach the student rather than reacting to the undesired behavior harshly. Being positive is knowing that behavioral change materializes through the teacher's competence, emotional support, and sensitivity (Allday, 2018; Ratcliff et al., 2010).

A positive attitude toward misbehaviors results in the following:

- Teachers understand that any number of variables in and outside the classroom could be causing the student to misbehave.
- Teachers know that their current classroom management plan can be modified when a rule, routine, or procedure is triggering behavioral problems. Teachers are flexible with the management plan, in other words.
- Teachers understand that students need to be taught specific social and functional skills.
- Teachers collaborate with school specialists to respond to the child's needs.
- Teachers collaborate with their Response to Intervention (RtI)/MTSS team to plan for levels of intervention that define, teach, and support student behaviors that meet schoolwide expectations.

In other words, teachers exercise patience and flexibility and adjust their management practices after understanding why, when, where, and how children misbehave (Ruef et al., 1998). Figure 2.1 shows more tips to help with classroom management.

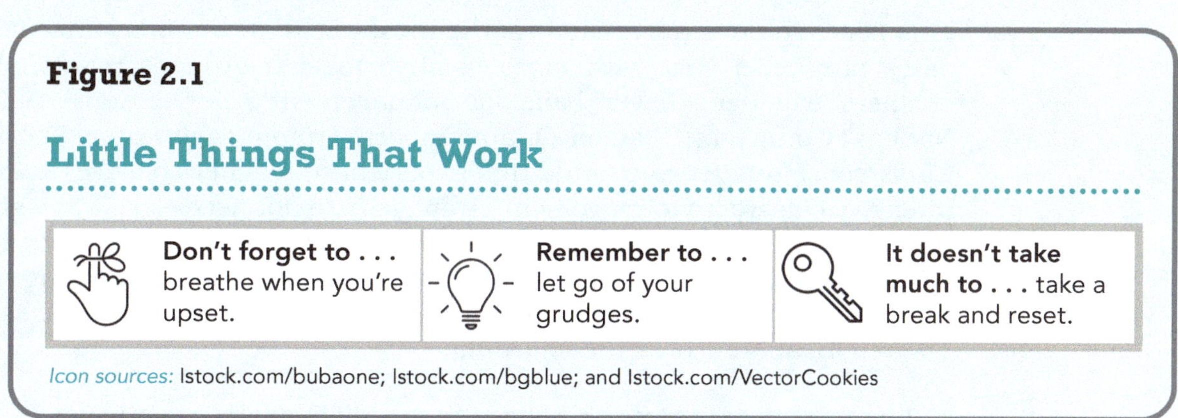

Positive practices and interventions are focused on giving clear directions, responding to the needs of students, and creating structured, predictable learning environments. We would like to add that teachers who maintain a positive approach react to rule violators calmly and consistently, they maintain control of the classroom, and they believe that a child's misbehavior can be replaced with appropriate behaviors that achieve the same purpose (Coy & Kostewicz, 2018; Lara, 2020).

Building Relationships Is Important

A positive approach especially encompasses building relationships with students. Most people would agree that teacher-student relationships are important to both students and teachers. What may not be immediately apparent is that those relationships have a positive impact on classroom management. Research has found that teachers who had high-quality relationships with students had almost one-third fewer discipline problems, rule violations, or other problems than teachers who did not (Marzano et al., 2003). In fact, research shows that caring and trusting relationships are critical not just for reducing behavior problems but for learning (Barron & Kinney, 2021). Students in positive relationships with teachers have been shown to improve their academic performance, increase their engagement in lessons, and increase their motivation and self-direction (Barron & Kinney, 2021).

It's never too early to start relationship building. Rimm-Kaufmann and Sandilos (2015), for instance, mention the positive impact that teacher-student relationships have on school adjustment, academic, and social performance. They report that some of the specific indicators related to behavior include less conflict, better social skills, more cooperation, and greater engagement in learning. Because this book focuses on elementary teachers, it is important for teachers to understand that early relationships between students and teachers have a lasting impact. When young children have more closeness and less conflict with teachers in kindergarten, they develop better social skills through eighth grade than those students with more conflict and less closeness (Rimm-Kaufmann & Sandilos, 2015).

This last reference to research is the most exciting to us, because it validates our belief that with more positive teacher-student relationships, teachers will need fewer behavior management interventions. A 2013 National Council on Teacher Quality report, *Training Our Future Teachers: Classroom Management*, found that experienced teachers believe that more intensive classroom management strategies are not necessary when strong relationships are built with students. They refer to other behavior management strategies, which we address in chapter 3, including using rules, routines, praise, responding to misbehavior, and increasing engagement. The report underscores the following:

> Virtually all teachers . . . believe that building relationships with students is just as essential for a functional, productive classroom as anything mentioned above, and that these relationships

can preclude the need for heavy-handed classroom management . . . Research indicates that effective teacher-student relationships are not established by teachers taking on a "buddy" role. Rather, teachers build relationships by providing clear purpose and strong guidance—the types of purpose and guidance that are conveyed by fair rules and productive routines, as well as by clear learning goals and expectations. (p. 5)

Simply put, children need to know that teachers care about them if they are expected to learn. This is especially true of students who may not have other support systems in their lives or whose families are not connected to their communities. When students trust that teachers know and care about them, there is a foundation for positive classroom behavior and experiences. As a teacher, you can build relationships with your students in a number of ways:

Call students by their name and use their names consistently during instruction and when greeting them. This is especially important when you have students from a culture or country other than your own. Don't assume. Take the time to learn how to pronounce students' names correctly, by asking them or their parents, and ask students at the beginning of the year if they prefer a nickname or use another name. Using name tags for a few days for everyone is a good way for you to learn all your students' names and for them to get to know each other.

Greet your students with a smile. Say "hi," offer a fist bump or a handshake, or ask "How are you today?" as students enter the classroom. Ask students which greeting they prefer and do whatever it is with a smile. Some teachers offer a menu of options and let students choose their greeting each day as the following figure 2.2 illustrates.

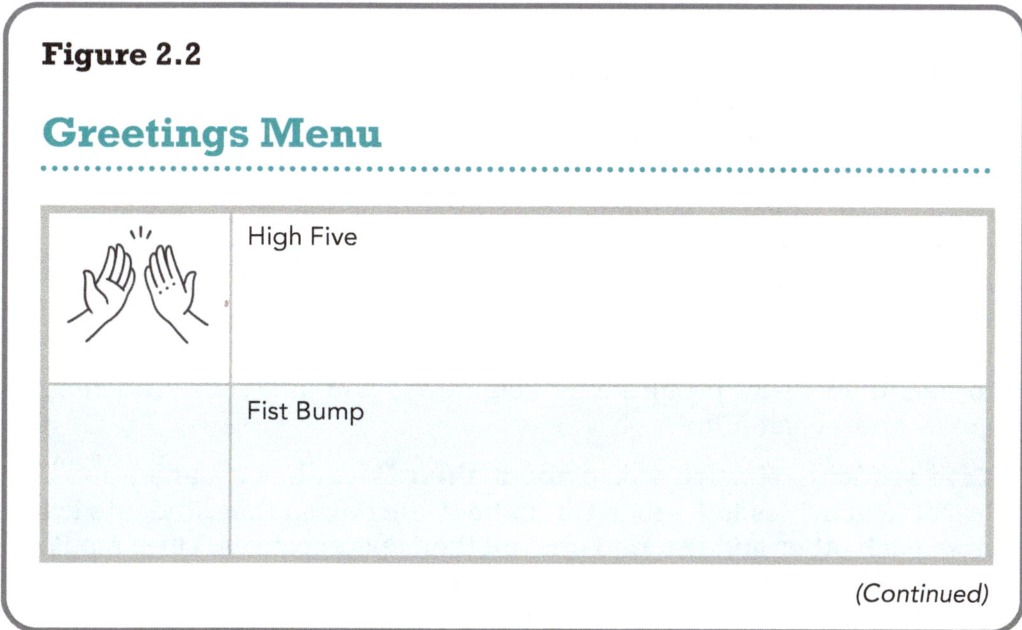

Figure 2.2

Greetings Menu

	High Five
	Fist Bump

(Continued)

(Continued)

	Hug
	Handshake
	Say Hello

Icon source: istock.com/snipergraphic, istock.com/appleuzr, Istock.com/ Catur Nurhadi, Istock .com/Sudowoodo, Istock.com/Turac Novruzova

Express how happy you are to know your students. Make comments such as, "I'm so glad you're in my class," "I'm happy that you're here," and "I'm lucky to have such great students." It is important that these comments are genuine. Students can usually tell if you mean what you are saying. We once knew a teacher who said she always found something positive to say about every single student. Sometimes, when she was tired or upset, it was difficult, but she still made sure to compliment, praise, or encourage each student individually, by name, every day. Doing so is worth the effort.

Take an interest in students' lives. Ask questions about students' likes and interests, what they like to do for fun, and how they spend their time with loved ones. While one-to-one time is difficult to find in busy classrooms, finding a few minutes each day or week to listen to individual students is one of the best ways to build a relationship. Some students may have parents who are not always at home or who are busy with jobs and other children. For those students, just having someone who will listen to them is important. Keep in mind that interest surveys, "all about me" forms, and learner profiles offer some ways you and your students get to know each other.

Give students time to share about their lives. Use collaborative learning activities in lessons throughout the day so that students learn from each other and listen to one another's perspectives. Offer regular opportunities for students to socialize and get to know each other. Students appreciate being able to talk during snack or free time or

Have each student fill out an interest survey. Attach their pictures, and then string them together for a display on a wall. Attach their pictures, and then string them together for a display on a wall as figure 2.3 shows.

Figure 2.3

Showcase of Student Interest

Image source: Istock.com/ Vitalii Petrushenko

share about their lives through a bulletin board that features aspects about their families and their interests. You could host a Classroom Café, where students get to spend a few minutes drinking from their water bottles and chit-chatting. Alternatively, group students together at lunch and at recess, and call it Lunch Bunch. Or, create a stack of cards, each with a question that students answer about themselves. When students are paired for an activity, give pairs a moment to draw a card and answer the question before beginning the main activity. Below is a list of questions that could be printed on the cards:

- Who's your favorite superhero? Why?
- What's your favorite movie? Why?
- What famous person would like to meet? Why?
- What's your favorite place to be? Why?
- What's your favorite toy? Why?
- What's your favorite thing to do on the weekend? Why?
- What pets do you wish you had? Why?

- What's your favorite restaurant? Why?
- If you could go anywhere in the world, where would you go, with whom, and why?

Publicize student accomplishments and celebrations from their lives. For example, say, "Way to go at the baseball game" or "I heard about your award in PE! That's awesome." You can also post students' classwork, artwork, and other achievements around the room. It's important to share with parents as well. We found a great idea online that suggests naming a bulletin board "The Fridge" as figure 2.4 shows. Display student work on that board at school, then encourage students to take their work home to display on their own fridges.

Figure 2.4

"The Fridge"

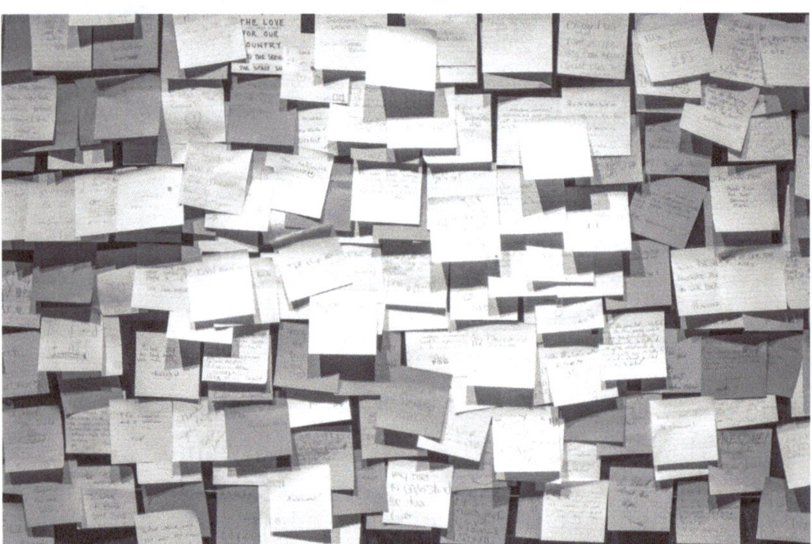

Image source: Istock.com/eyfoto

Check in on individual students who may need some extra attention. Ask how students are doing, if they need any academic help, or if they need some advice to deal with a challenge they are experiencing. The better you know the student, the more likely it is that you will "read" them and know when they need help. But it is always a good idea to check in with students individually. Some students' cultures, backgrounds, or personalities discourage asking questions or asking for help. With those students, do this quietly and privately if possible.

The big takeaway about relationships for teachers is this: When students have trusting relationships with their teachers, they will feel they are special and that they belong in the classroom and school, which, in turn, will encourage them to behave and perform to the level of expectation. This book focuses on prevention of misbehavior as well as intervention, and we view all these outcomes of strong teacher-student relationships not just as healthy and positive but also as directly linked to misbehavior prevention.

CLASSROOM CONNECTION

Students of diverse abilities and cultures are more likely to work together when the classroom climate is one where they feel respected and connected. To develop a positive attitude toward everyone, one teacher uses the cheer chain as seen in figure 2.5. She selects a behavior or social skill to target, and when she notices a student exemplifying it, she gives him a chain and the whole class cheers for the student. Then, when that student sees a classmate performing the same action, he passes it on and the class cheers again.

Figure 2.5

The Cheer Chain

Image source: Bridget Zimmerman. Used with permission.

Proactive Behavior Management Practices

In this book, we use the term *proactive* for two reasons. First, to suggest that teachers recognize that children misbehave because they have social and functional skill deficiencies. Second, to show that because teachers can anticipate why, when, where, and how the misbehavior occurs, they can teach students appropriate skills to prevent the behavior or keep it from escalating (Moreno & Bullock, 2011). In other words, proactive practices are preplanned efforts to prevent misbehavior (Hirsch et al., 2019). Proactive educators identify and teach cognitive behavioral competencies that are designed to develop appropriate school behaviors that help children participate in instructional activities successfully. These competencies include the following:

- Executive functioning skills, such as problem solving, attentiveness and concentration, and task persistence
- Emotional regulation skills, such as emotional awareness, self-control, and stress management
- Social communications and interactions skills, such as sharing, using manners, and respecting personal space. (Diperna et al., 2016)

Our interventions for specific behavior problems are designed to teach and maintain these skills. Beyond specific interventions, though, proactive practices can be used in a number of ways.

CLASSROOM ARRANGEMENTS

Allowing students to share in the decision-making process promotes a sense of ownership and belonging, which reduces stress and other behavioral issues (Frieberg et al., 2009). Teachers who embrace a proactive approach to the classroom community invite students to contribute to the classroom's rules, routines, and seating arrangements (Stichter et al., 2009). Consider asking students to name your class (e.g., The Mighty Mustangs), reciting a daily pledge together, having students write their own class norms, or offering multiple ways to use classroom spaces, for example. When one teacher asked her third graders what they wanted as a positive reinforcement, she anticipated that they would propose edible treats. But her students surprised her. Their suggestions included assigning themselves a nickname to be used by the teacher and their peers throughout the day, bringing a favorite stuffed animal from home and keeping it at their desk for the day, and changing desks for the day. She noticed that their behaviors improved because they wanted to choose one of their own suggested rewards!

BEHAVIORAL EXPECTATIONS

Having clear behavioral expectations and reviewing them regularly encourages students to behave appropriately. In other words, a proactive practice is to remind students of appropriate behaviors before they misbehave. At the beginning of lessons, for example, you might say, "Let me see you sitting up straight with your desks cleared off and your eyes on me." During a lesson, you can add, "I want you to quietly pair up with your elbow partner and explain how you would solve this math problem. In two minutes, I'll call on a pair to show me their work." At the end of a lesson, you could say,

"Thank you for working quietly with your partners. Give each other a soft high five. I'm going to give you two minutes to walk to your desks and take out your social studies books." Another proactive strategy is to inform or remind students about your noise level expectations. You might say, "We will be walking quietly in the hallway, so voices off," or "Remember to whisper in your groups because the teacher next door is giving her class a test."

INSTRUCTION

Designing and delivering instruction that is fun and personable, and that integrates relatable examples, also reduces behavior challenges (Billingsley, 2016). Scott et al. (2001) explain, "The student who is successful with and enjoys an activity has little incentive to disrupt the class or to act in ways which would precipitate [their] exclusion from the activity—and in fact [has] been found to have more appropriate social behaviors" (p. 316). A proactive practice also gives the students some control over assignments, activities, and assessments. Billingsley (2016) adds, "Simply allowing students to choose the order in which learning tasks are to be presented or completed offers reluctant learners a sense of control in their learning" (p. 14).

When the content is difficult or unwelcoming for students, consider rewarding the students with a fun activity at the end of the lesson. First, share at the beginning of the lesson what the activity will be—such as five minutes to talk quietly with a buddy, draw with markers, or design a fun bulletin board—then teach the lesson and follow through with the reinforcement. The idea is that students will sincerely attempt the instruction because they know they are going to do something fun at the end.

Following are some additional ideas for keeping students engaged, on task, and working toward meeting their goals.

- **Get all students' attention at the beginning of the lesson.** Personalize the content by using their names (*Jason, did you know that when your grandma cuts up her delicious cake, she's using fractions?*), relating it to their background and experiences (*Maria, when you went to the zoo, what did you notice about the chimps? Today, we're going to learn about Jane Goodall and how she did research.),* and explaining why the content or skill they are learning is important.
- **Make the content interesting to students.** Augment lectures with anchor and reference charts, vibrant visuals and images, live webcams (cities, zoos, aquariums, beaches, and sanctuaries often feature live scenery and animals), and videos.
- **Ask critical thinking questions to spark conversations about the subject matter, in pairs, small groups, or with the whole class.** Switch up groups and partners throughout the day so students get to talk with different classmates.
- **Present students with objects** (e.g., owl pellets, coins, plants), **artifacts** (e.g., art, jewelry, pictures), **and materials** (e.g., copies of

political cartoons, quotes, drawings) **they can explore by answering critical thinking questions about them**.

- **Use total participation techniques that expect *all* students to move around the classroom.** Strategies such as Scoot!, Four Corners, and Gallery Walk require students to work together and share ideas as they tour exhibits and respond to critical thinking questions.
- **Give specific praise and positive feedback as students work.** Providing students with information about what they do right encourages them to demonstrate those behaviors continuously.
- **Close the lesson with the transition in mind.** Students tend to become disruptive during transitions. For this reason, warn students about how much time they have remaining in the lesson (*We have two minutes before we start science*); give instructions with three or fewer steps (*Make sure your name is on your paper and hand it to your table captain who will put in the writing folder*); and explain how you expect them ready for the next lesson (*In one minute, be in the* Ready to Learn *position with a clear desk*).

Prosocial Behavior Management Practices

When we use the term *prosocial practices*, we mean teaching students interpersonal skills to use in the classroom. Children come to school with different levels of social skills. Many need help learning how to work with others, which encompasses the conventions associated with respect, cooperation, care, and encouragement, among others. Some may need help with emotional competencies such as self-regulation, self-management, decision-making, and social awareness. Other children may lack more basic peer-related social skills, such as smiling, making eye contact, nodding, approaching others, and so on, which makes it difficult for them to make and keep friends, work effectively with their classmates, and cope with the demands of socializing at lunch or recess. This increases these students' risks for developing internalizing and externalizing behavior problems (Herbert-Myers et al., 2006). Conversely, students who have good social skills have more positive attitudes about school and better relationships with their peers (POWER-Solving, 2022; Shamnadh & Anzari, 2019).

In all, being prosocial means promoting social and emotional skills that are incompatible with problem behaviors. To successfully use prosocial practices, first identify an important social skill to teach. Then model the skill (e.g., "Smile when you greet someone"), allow for plenty of practice (e.g., "Let's practice in pairs here and when we see someone when we're in the hallway), and then reinforce when it is demonstrated (e.g., "It was so nice to see you smile at Emilio."). In some instances, consider teaching social skills instructions individually or in small groups. Table 2.1 presents some important social skills to consider teaching, depending on the needs of your students.

Table 2.1

Consider Teaching These Social Skills

SOCIAL SKILLS	HOW TO:
Basic	Make eye contact Smile Greet someone Read facial cues and body language
Approach Others	Walk up to someone Start a conversation Keep conversations going Communicate clearly Ask or say things nicely Maintain personal space
Work with Others	Use kind words Use an appropriate voice level Take turns Listen to others Give compliments Encourage others Negotiate/compromise Participate and contribute Disagree politely Deal with problems and conflicts
Manners	Say please and thank you Be polite and considerate Share books, supplies, and materials Offer help Admit wrongdoing and apologize
Manage Emotions and Reactions	Express feelings appropriately Express point of view kindly Demonstrate sportsmanship Express anger and frustration appropriately Deal with worry and anxiety appropriately Use coping strategies

Pow! How? Now!	
	What are your reactions to what you read so far?
	How will you use this information that you just read?
	What does this information mean, especially with your most challenging students?

Icon source: Istock.com/nazarkru and Istock.com/lineartestpilot

PART II

PREVENTING MISBEHAVIORS

CHAPTER 3

ESTABLISH YOUR BEHAVIOR MANAGEMENT SYSTEM

What's in This Chapter

- Establish Clear Rules
- Use a System of Consequences
- Communicate Positively
- Be Assertive, Consistent, and Respectful

Your Needs and Wants

I need recommendations for preventing misbehaviors. I want some ideas for setting up my behavior management system.

Questions to Think About as You Read the Chapter

- How effective are your rules for preventing misbehaviors?
- How well do your students know your classroom procedures?
- How would you describe your communication style with your students?

The last chapter covered three approaches to behavior management that work to improve student behavior. To further reduce the likelihood of recurring misbehaviors, you need to establish a behavior management system that supports a positive learning environment. Here, you will read about practices associated with behavioral expectations and consequences. Structured rules, routines, and procedures that are consistently applied let students know how you expect them to learn in the classroom. They hold students accountable for their behavior and let them know what your boundaries are.

Establish Clear Rules

Your classroom should be structured and predictable, a learning environment with routines, firm expectations, and limited surprises and/or drastic changes to procedures. Students are less likely to misbehave when they know what to expect and do. Having clear and concise rules is an essential practice that contributes to structure and predictability.

Classroom rules are your behavioral expectations for students across lessons, activities, and settings. The clearer they are, the better. Establish rules that are developmentally appropriate, succinct, and consistent with school expectations (Zoromski et al., 2021). Create at least a few rules (three to five is usually manageable for elementary students) that remind students what *to* do rather than what *not* to do (e.g., *walk* instead of *don't run*).

Below are some rules that we have seen in classrooms. Take a moment to reflect on how the vague rules lack the information students need to fully understand the teacher's behavioral expectations as the following figure 3.1 illustrates.

Figure 3.1

Do's and Don'ts of Classroom Rules

VAGUE	CLEAR
Be respectful.	Keep hands, feet, and objects to yourself.
Be honest.	Raise your hand to ask and answer teacher questions.
Obey adults.	Use kind words with your classmates.
Work hard.	Keep your area clean.
Use books and materials appropriately.	Return classroom supplies where they belong.
Do your best.	Say please and thank you.
Believe in yourself.	

Post your classroom rules in a prominent location where they can be seen and easily referenced. Then, teach and reteach the rules the first day, week, and month, and continue to address them throughout the school year to support and encourage desired behaviors. During these lessons, discuss why rules are important. Take a moment to explain the purpose of each rule in ways that students will understand. For example, "Our first rule is to *raise your hand if you have a question or want to make a comment.* Why would we have this rule?

What would happen if we all spoke out at once?" After listening to the students' answers, continue: "When you raise your hand before speaking out loud, everyone has a chance to participate. Sometimes I might wait a few seconds before calling on someone, because I want you to think about your answers rather than calling out the first thought that jumps into your head." The rationale for each rule should be reasonable and acceptable to students. Students will have a hard time following a rule if it's one they don't understand. Use this time to talk about character traits such as respect, responsibility, kindness, and trust, which underpin the prosocial behaviors presented in chapter 2.

Use students' feedback to revise the rules—if applicable—so that they meet students' unique contributions and needs. Afterward, explicitly model appropriate rule following. For example: *I'm going to pretend that I'm a student and I have a question. I raise my hand and I wait for the teacher to call on me. I stay quiet until the teacher says my name, then I speak.* Then have the students practice asking questions, lining up, turning in work, and so forth. As Hirsch et al. (2019) emphasize, "Active practice of classroom expectations has produced increased engagement and reduced disruptive behavior" (p. 63).

CLASSROOM CONNECTION

When inviting students to revise the classroom rules, start with some basic ones first as a guideline for the desired behaviors. Then, ask the students for their input (e.g., "What does this rule mean to you?"). Here is an example of how a class might rework a basic rule in figure 3.2:

Figure 3.2

Basic Rules and Revised Rules

BASIC RULE	REVISED RULE
Use kind words with your classmates	We greet each other with "Hello" and ask, "How are you?" We say nice things about our classmates We encourage our classmates when they are struggling
Keep your area clean	We throw away trash We keep our desks neat We put away materials when we finish using them
Say please and thank you	We say please, thank you, and you're welcome We say "bless you" when someone sneezes We say "excuse me"

After you've discussed, revised, and practiced the rules, regularly review them and reinforce rule-following behaviors. Here are a few examples:

- "Thank you, Joaquin, Mary, and Joslyn, for following the rule of raising your hands."
- "When you work with your partners, follow the rule of using your inside voices."
- "Megan, Kyle, and Marc, nice job of following the rule of standing quietly while we wait in the hallway."
- "I'm noticing Jake following our rule of sitting in the learner's position. Great job."
- "Thank you, Pablo, for following our rule of respecting our library books."
- "As you get started, remember our rule *We do not disturb others when they are working.*"

The last step of using rules effectively is to enforce them consistently so that students know what to do at all times. The more consistent you are, the more predictable the classroom becomes. When a student breaks a rule, it is best to respond immediately with a follow-up action or a consequence. Zoromski et al. (2019) explain, "Recent research conducted in elementary classrooms indicated that [a higher] percentage of rule violations appropriately responded to by the teacher . . . was associated with lower rates of disruptive behavior" (p. 202). There will be times when you will have students with behavioral challenges and their misbehaviors seem to spread. This can be challenging for new teachers. At these moments, don't be afraid to stop class and give the students a short break (e.g., two or three minutes). Consider using some of the calming techniques that are found in chapter 4, such as deep breathing or visualization exercises. But more importantly, this is the time to review the rules and behavioral consequences. In addition, consider a private conversation with the student who seems to be encouraging others to misbehave.

A FEW WORDS ABOUT RULE VIOLATIONS AND CONSEQUENCES

When students do not follow classroom rules, routines, and other social conventions, we suggest the hierarchy of follow-up actions and consequences described below. If a student persists with misbehavior, continue through the whole list. Otherwise, stop at the point where the student begins to meet the desired behavior.

After reading *Enemy Pie* by Derek Munson, students are assigned to write a paragraph on what makes a friend. Jason is procrastinating. He's fiddling with his school box; getting up to sharpen his pencil, drink some water, and grab an object from his cubby;

showing his tablemates his bandage; and talking to the student seated behind him. See examples of follow-up consequences in figure 3.3.

Figure 3.3

Follow-Up Consequences and Examples

FOLLOW-UP ACTIONS/ CONSEQUENCES	EXAMPLES
1 – Redirect the student to the expected behavior.	"Jason, start writing your heading on your paper and work on your first sentence. I'll swing by in a moment to help you structure your thesis statement."
2 – Announce the rule.	"Remember our class rule: when we have a class assignment, we work quietly so that our classmates can finish their work."
3 – Announce your behavioral expectations when you see the student breaking the rule again.	"I see some of you working hard on your paragraphs. Thank you. You should have at least two sentences written down. If you finish early, you can create an invitation for your friend to visit and play with you."
4 – Walk over to the student's space and support them. Remind them about the class rule and your expectations.	"Okay, Jason, show me what you have." After working with him, say, "Remember, when students have an assignment to work on, we work quietly too, so we don't disrupt them. Now, write the next two sentences on your own."
5 – Take the student to an area for a quick private conversation where you can still see the whole class.	"Jason, come with me into the hallway for a moment."
• Explain what you observed (e.g., what you saw, heard) and the consequences of the actions.	• "I noticed you moving around a lot and disrupting your tablemates. Even though you were whispering, sometimes you were loud enough for the whole class to hear. When you walk around, talk, and fiddle loudly through your belongings, you keep others from finishing their work, and that's not fair to them. That's why we have the rule."
• Ask how they are feeling and solicit suggestions to improve the behavior.	• "What's going on? How are you feeling? What can we do so that you have a good day? How can I help you?"
• Consider providing them some options.	• "How about you choose someone to walk with you down to the end of the hallway and back and share with each other why you enjoy your favorite toy. When you come back, if you need a little help getting back on task, just raise your hand and I'll come help."
• Ask the student to return to their seat and honor the rule.	• "When we get back inside, go to your seat and remember our rule as you work."

(Continued)

(Continued)

An important note: You can't use this hierarchy for all rule violations, because it is *never* okay for children to deliberately hurt one another through intimidation, coercion, insults, and other forms of violence. When students harm or threaten others with physical abuse and aggression, immediate disciplinary action is *the* consequence. So, when serious offenses occur, office referrals and conferencing with parents are applicable consequences. Follow your school policies and procedures for infractions involving dangerous offenses, weapons, drugs, and fighting. While the punishment might not change the child's behavior, it does convey that students' safety and security is important and they are protected from harm's way.

You should also consider the demands of the specific assignment and the amount of time and attention provided to one student. When a student's behavior takes so much time away from instruction that it interferes with other students' learning or monopolizes your time, you might want to implement a sequence that is shorter. For example, in this situation, if Jason fails to respond and other students become restless or they need your assistance, you could say to Jason, "Jason, please move to the quiet area. After I help some other students, I will come work with you." Then, move ahead with the sequence of steps in the example.

Use a System of Consequences

Well-designed consequences can change students' behavior, but only if they are used appropriately and implemented consistently. Here are some guidelines:

- **Consequences should be respectful of an individual student, the teacher, and other students in the classroom.** Consequences should not be mean-spirited, sarcastic, demeaning, or disproportionate. When implementing a consequence, teachers should be calm and fair and should convey respect for the student.
- **Consequences for misbehaviors should be designed to be corrective and reductive.** When a student misbehaves, the consequence should teach a prosocial behavior to replace it. If the consequence is intended to reduce the frequency or quality of a behavior, then, over time, there should be evidence that it is working—the behavior is less frequent, less severe, or interferes less with teaching and learning.
- **Consequences should occur both after positive, prosocial behaviors and after problematic, interfering misbehaviors.** Attention is powerful. Use it to let students know when their behavior is positive and prosocial.

- **Use consequences consistently.** The more that students know what to expect and that their teacher's actions are reliable and predictable, the more trust they will have and the more effective the consequences will be. Part of consistency is not threatening to do something, just saying or doing it.

To design a system of consequences, think first about the behaviors that you want to respond to in your management system. For example, which behaviors are most important? How many behaviors do you want in your system? Do they make sense? Are you comfortable with them? We suggest that you focus on behaviors that (a) are most essential for a positive classroom, (b) are easy to evaluate (is the student demonstrating the behavior or not?), (c) help create an environment that allows for teaching and learning, and (d) are positive and prosocial. Are there some minor misbehaviors that you are choosing to ignore? Are you sure about those? The consequences system you end up with should not try to address every misbehavior that might occur in the classroom. Prioritize.

Next, think about both positive consequences and reductive/corrective consequences. Always consider your district or campus guidelines for consequences first. Then, think about the qualities of the consequences. Will the students have input into them? Are they reasonable and easy to implement? If a student demonstrates a positive behavior, the consequence can be verbal, tangible, immediate, private, choice based, personal, enjoyable, and many other qualities. The consequences for misbehaviors should be carefully considered as well: Will they be private? Are they simply punishment or will they teach the acceptable alternative behavior? Are they quick and easy to use? Do they seem fair? Are they consistent but still flexible?

Finally, start small. Use a simple, basic framework first. Check with your students to be sure they understand what you mean by each behavior expectation. (Consider using a Looks Like/Sounds Like chart for this.) Additionally, make sure that everyone understands the consequences. For the consequences to work, they must matter to students. If they don't understand or care about the consequences, do not use them.

In addition to a Looks Like/Sounds Like chart, a consequences chart is useful. A quick online search will yield many examples of consequence charts, often taken directly from classrooms. Before you design your own, consider the examples you see online. Think about which ones match your priorities, your style of teaching, and, most importantly, the needs of your students. What behaviors do they need to learn? How can you best support them as they learn those behaviors? Consider the example in figure 3.4 of a consequence system. Remember that you are teaching behaviors, so you are likely to have more consequences for positive, prosocial behaviors than for misbehaviors. Note that while the group can be collectively rewarded with positive consequences for meeting behavior expectations, they should never be collectively punished for one student's misbehavior.

Figure 3.4

Target Goal: Be Respectful to Each Other

RESPECTFUL BEHAVIORS	CONSEQUENCES FOR POSITIVE, PROSOCIAL BEHAVIORS	CONSEQUENCES FOR MISBEHAVIORS
"WHAT DO THE BEHAVIORS LOOK LIKE?"	**"WHAT SHOULD HAPPEN IF MEET OUR TARGET GOAL?"**	**"WHAT SHOULD HAPPEN IF A STUDENT IS NOT RESPECTFUL?"**
We use words such as "Please," "Thank you," and "Excuse me."	We get respect tickets that we can trade in for eating lunch in the classroom, GoNoodle® time, or a Friday popcorn party.	The student pauses a few minutes to reflect on their behavior and then shows how they should behave.
We listen quietly when the teacher or another student is talking.	We get an extra five minutes at recess.	The student apologizes to the students or teachers they were disrespectful to. The student can write their apology and say it.
We follow rules and directions.	We get a homework pass.	The student watches and compliments at least three students who are being respectful.
We raise our hands when we have a question or we have something to say.	The teacher calls our families and says nice things about our behavior.	Have a five-minute follow-up conference; the teacher asks the students to explain to each other how disrespect makes them feel.
We help each other.	We applaud, do a silent cheer, or give group high fives.	The teacher refers the student to the counselor who can help them work on social skills.

Communicate Positively

Positive communication includes praise, positive feedback, and giving directions in a manner that makes them likely to be followed. All three help reinforce expected classroom behaviors.

PRAISE

Before we discuss using praise in the classroom, we should note that some teachers do not like to praise children because they deem it unnecessary; because they are convinced it creates children who eagerly expect it; or because they believe praise does not reflect real-world conditions (for example, adults do not get praised for following the law). Of course, there are children who willingly follow directions, complete assigned tasks, and fulfill teacher expectations without the need for praise. Whatever directive they fulfill is the reward itself. But many students need regular praise and positive feedback to develop the social, learning, or behavioral skills they need to succeed in the classroom (Ruef et al., 1998). And all students love being appreciated. If you are among the teachers who do not like to use praise, we urge you to reconsider.

We define *praise* as a favorable verbal statement (e.g., "Way to go!") or nonverbal gesture (e.g., a thumbs-up or a high five) directed at students who are behaving appropriately. Praise conveys teacher approval of the desired student behavior and gives encouragement to continue behaving as expected. Some research has found that as rates of praise in the classroom increase, student disruptions decrease (Downs et al., 2019). Our own experiences have taught us that when some students earn praise, other students begin to demonstrate the behaviors they see the teacher rewarding. Ratcliff et al. (2010) add, "Something as simple as saying, 'Thank you for making a wise choice,' may have a powerful impact on every student in the classroom" (p, 213).

There are two types of praise: general and specific. General praise does not target or address explicit desired behaviors. Specific praise, on the other hand, describes the positive behavior that the student demonstrated (Sobeck & Reister, 2021). Figure 3.5 shows some examples of praise. Notice how general praise leaves some doubt of what the child did to receive it, but the specific praise lets the student know exactly what she did right.

Figure 3.5

Examples of Praise

GENERAL PRAISE	SPECIFIC PRAISE
Nice job!	Nice job writing your heading and numbering your paper!
Well done!	Well done taking turns on the math problems!
Excellent!	Excellent way of encouraging your group to pay attention to what I was about to say.

Specific praise is more effective in shaping students' behaviors because it confirms understanding, improves understanding, or clarifies misunderstanding (Owens et al., 2018; Whitney & Ackerman, 2020). However, for praise to be beneficial, it must be sincere, be explicit, and immediately follow the desired behavior's occurrence (Simpson et al., 2020). Moreover, when praising a student, avoid describing their abilities, using phrases such as *You are so smart*, *You're good at everything*, and *You're awesome at math.* Whitney and Ackerman (2020) explain that "when a teacher praises a student on his or her improvement or effort, it is a much more fluid process. The student can relate the statement to their individual goals, the progress toward those goals, and what needs to be done to improve their progress" (p, 88).

POSITIVE FEEDBACK

Positive feedback provides students with additional information to maintain or improve their performance, and it focuses on what the teacher wants to see demonstrated continuously. Here are some things to keep in mind when giving positive feedback:

- Identify in advance the times to provide feedback rather than waiting for the student to elicit it from you (e.g., "Miss, did you see how I . . . ?) (Whitney & Ackerman, 2020).
- Provide it as soon as the behavior occurs (Sobeck & Reister, 2021).
- Get the student's attention by saying their name (Owens et al., 2018).
- Describe the behavior that is meeting your expectations (Närhi et al., 2017).
- Make sure that the feedback is sincere. Whitney and Ackerman (2020) explain, "If a student views the feedback as genuine, it may promote a positive teacher-student relationship, which has been shown to reduce externalizing behaviors" (p. 90).
- Add praise to show you appreciate positive behavior (Ruef et al., 1998).

Figure 3.6 shows examples of how to add positive feedback to your specific praise.

Figure 3.6

Adding Positive Feedback

SPECIFIC PRAISE	POSITIVE FEEDBACK
Great job raising your hand!	Jeremy, thank you for raising your hand and waiting patiently for me to call on you.
Excellent! You walked quietly in the hallway.	Rocio, excellent job of walking with your hands to your side and keeping your voice quiet.
You were awesome during reading!	Joaquin, you stayed on your square during reading with your hands folded across your lap just like I asked. That's awesome!
Fantastic job of lining up after lunch!	Maggie, I noticed that you lined up quickly when you heard the whistle blow. Fantastic job!

Source: Adapted from Simpson, Hopkins, Eakle, and Rose, 2020.

DIRECTIONS THAT ARE LIKELY TO BE FOLLOWED

Clear communication increases the chances of directions being followed. Thirty years of research has shown effective ways of directing student behavior (Ratcliff et al., 2010). So that students follow your directions, consider these guidelines:

- Include only as many steps as needed. For example, say "Sit down and number your paper from one to three" rather than "Sit down, be quiet, get out your paper, number it from one to three, and stay seated quietly the whole time."
- Similarly, give single directions at a time. For example, "Put your crayons in the cubby" is more effective than "Stop what you're doing. Go back to your seats. You should have nothing on your desk. So, if the crayons are out, put them in the cubby."
- Use initiating rather than terminating directions. In other words, the directions should ask the student to start a behavior rather than stop it. For example, say "Start writing your paragraph" rather than "Stop messing with your pencil and get to work."
- Give specific directions (for example, "Put your pencils down and look at me" instead of "Pay attention." And "Push in your chairs, and line up without talking" instead of "Line up!").
- Allow enough time for students to follow your directions. Five to ten seconds of wait time is sufficient for the student to respond or begin the expected behavior.
- When giving directions to a specific student, wait until you are near the student rather than shouting from across the room.
- Get the student's attention (by making eye contact or saying their name) before giving the directions.

Be Assertive, Consistent, and Respectful

Finally, as you establish your behavior management system and work toward preventing misbehaviors, stay the leader, always. To that end, maintain confidence, determination, honesty, patience, firmness, courage, and leadership. Students are more likely to get out of control and take over class when teachers are weak or doubtful about their management skills. Ratcliff and her colleagues (2010) point out that strong teachers from Phil Schlechty's (1970) classic study "observed students to see that directives were being followed; they exhibited a calm confidence; . . . [and] they avoided confrontations in front of the class. . . . They rarely used threatening comments. . . . [Instead,] the teacher paused, watching while the student complied, and then continued with the experience" (p. 311). Maintain clear boundaries between you and your students and recognize that you are their teacher, not their friend. Babkie (2006) explains that when "boundaries become blurred . . . this can lead to student uncertainty about classroom limits and an increased likelihood of potential management problems" (p. 184).

Develop the habit of scanning the classroom continuously. Make eye contact with students to prevent problems before they materialize. Jacob Kounin called this *withitness*, which refers to the ability to forecast potential problems because a teacher is aware of what is going on at all times and their students know it (Fielstein & Phelps, 2001). As Ormrod et al. (2019) put it, when teachers are *withit*, "they know what misbehaviors are occurring *when* those misbehaviors occur, and they know who the perpetrators are" (p. 473).

Respect students at all times. Remember the adage *When we show respect for others, they respond with respect for us*, which is equally significant to children. Students will misbehave if they feel disrespected. Babkie (2006) suggests, "One way to analyze your level of respect is to consider how you wish to be treated and use that as a guideline in working with your students" (p. 187). Here are just a few ways to respect students:

- Treat all students fairly (abstain from treating students differently based on personal traits).
- Create fair rules and policies that apply to all students.
- Use a calm tone when responding to student misbehaviors (avoid shouting, shushing, or snapping fingers at students).
- Give directives without sarcasm or humiliation.
- Apologize when you make mistakes.
- Avoid retaliating against perpetrators.
- Use encouraging language that makes students feel comfortable, capable, and like contributing members of the classroom.

Pow! How? Now!	
POW!	What are your reactions to what you read so far?
HOW?	How will you use this information that you just read?
NOW!	What does this information mean, especially with your most challenging students?

Icon source: Istock.com/nazarkru and Istock.com/lineartestpilot

TEACH AND PRACTICE POSITIVE BEHAVIORAL SKILLS

CHAPTER 4

What's in This Chapter

- Model Behavioral Expectations
- Teach Academic Survival Skills
- Teach Self-Regulation Skills
- Teach Calming Techniques

Your Needs and Wants

I need to know what skills to teach my students to prevent misbehaviors. I want some ideas for teaching, modeling, and practicing skills that can help them self-manage their behavior.

Questions to Think About as You Read the Chapter

- How do you plan for meaningful instruction?
- What academic skills do your students need most? How do you teach them?
- What calming techniques and self-regulation skills help your students manage their behaviors?

In the last chapter we discussed what you should do first to prevent misbehaviors, which is to establish a system of expectations and consequences so that students know how you want them to behave. Established rules about procedures, routines, and behaviors inform your students about how they are expected to function in your classroom. Many students, however, will not follow your system simply because you expect them to. They need to be taught how to behave and manage themselves, so that they successfully participate in instruction, collaborate in learning activities, and work independently on classwork. Here, you will read about teaching and practicing positive behavioral skills to prevent misbehaviors from occurring.

Model Behavioral Expectations

Just as you model rule-following, demonstrate your expectations for behaviors not explicitly mentioned in your rules. Show students the academic and social-emotional skills that you expect to see. Some students need straightforward instruction with procedures associated with clearcut guidance outlined in figure 4.1.

Figure 4.1

Classroom Task Rules

	SOME QUESTIONS TO ASK YOURSELF
What to do at the beginning of lessons	Where are the students seated at the start of the lessons? What materials should they have ready? How should their desks look?
What to do during transitions from one lesson to the next	Are the students allowed to talk? What do they do with the materials and books from the prior lesson? Where do they turn in completed assignments? Can they use the restroom or fountain at this time?
When and how to access class supplies, materials, and books	How accessible are the supplies, materials, and books? Who distributes and collects them? Can they be accessed at any time?
When to use the pencil sharpener	How often can the students use the sharpener? Can any student use the sharpener or only designated students?
When to talk during lessons	When do you expect silence? When do you expect whispers, low voices, and conversational voice talking?
How to ask for help	How do they ask for help? When can they ask for help? When can classmates help each other?
When to use the restroom and drinking fountain	Can students leave the room without disturbing others? When can students visit the restroom and fountain? How many students are allowed to use the restroom or fountain during lessons?
Where to work on class assignments and group activities	Do the students work at their desks, or can they choose any space to work? Can they work on the floor? What spaces are designated for group work? What spaces are designated for independent work?

Posting and referencing a noise level chart like this one can help keep students from getting too loud.

Figure 4.2

Noise Level Chart

1	Quiet	 Shhh....
2	Whisper	
3	Talk quietly	
4	Loud Voice	
5	Outside Voice	

Image source: Istock.com/ lemono, Istock.com/ zuperia, Istock.com/ Colorfuel Studio, Istock.com/ Vera Kostyleva and Istock.com/ djvstock

Then, provide the students with plenty of opportunities to practice the skills. Rehearsals are critical for their success. For students who have an especially difficult time with any of these skills, consider using a Social Story™ (Gray, 1998), which "is a short story written in the first person that has been used to teach children the social expectations of situations in which they have presented behavioral difficulties. Stories have included information on who is involved, what is happening, how the child can respond, and how others may respond and feel. Narratives may be used to target nonverbal behavior (e.g., raising one's hand, following directions), verbal behavior (e.g., answering questions, greeting), or a combination (e.g., playing with a friend)" (Schneider & Goldstein, 2009, p. 250).

An example of a Social Story titled, *Talking with My Classmates.*

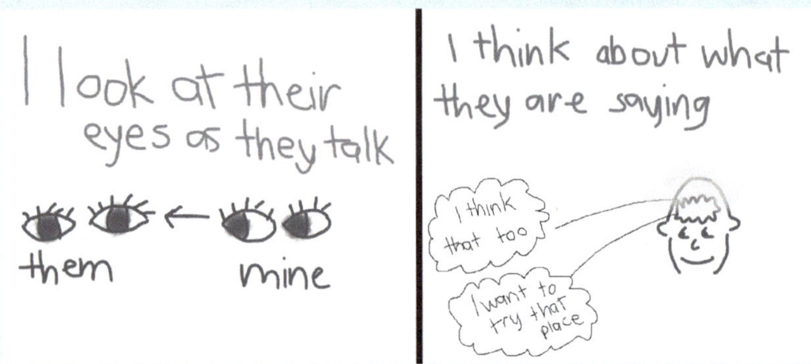

Teach Academic Survival Skills

The root cause of some students' misbehavior is often an academic issue. So, when students do not know how to tackle instructions, assignments, activities, projects, and so forth, they goof off, they get disrespectful, they become the class clown, and so forth. One 2018 study found that one out of five students disrupted or distracted the learning environment because they were frustrated with assignments (Johnson et al., 2019). To help improve students' academic development and reduce misbehaviors, teach and model literate behaviors found in the figure below. We know that this is a lot of teaching! Don't get overwhelmed with thinking these have to be taught all at once. Think of your students' unique needs and choose those skills that need the most attention. Work your way through the skills accordingly as suggested in figure 4.3.

Figure 4.3

Think-Aloud Examples of What Can Be Modeled

	THINK-ALOUD EXAMPLES OF WHAT CAN BE MODELED
How to complete assignments successfully	What paper, writing utensils, and books do I need? I'll read the instructions carefully. I'll make a mental plan of what I am going to do and how I'm going to do it. I'll raise my hand to ask clarification questions. I'll double-check my work before I turn it in.

	THINK-ALOUD EXAMPLES OF WHAT CAN BE MODELED
How to learn from a book	Read the title and headings; skim the pages before reading. Make connections to what I already know. Visualize what I am reading. Ask questions about what I am reading.
How to stay on task	Keep my eyes on the teacher. Listen to what she is saying. Make connections to what she is saying. Raise my hand to ask or answer questions.
When to raise hand	If I have a question about what the teacher is saying, I raise my hand. If I want to contribute to what the teacher is saying, I raise my hand. If I need permission, I raise my hand. If I have a need, I raise my hand and tell the teacher.
What to say instead of *I don't know*	If I don't know, I can ask my teacher (or classmate) the following: • Will you repeat the question? • May I have some more information? • May I ask a classmate to help? • May I have some time to think? • Can you tell me where I can find information to answer your question?
How to work with a partner	Greet my partner with a hi, hello, or a nod and a smile. Make eye contact. Listen to what they have to say, nodding to show you understand. Use an inside voice when we take turns sharing our thoughts. Ask questions or add to what they are saying. When I finish, I thank them.
How to work in a group	I sit with my group facing the members. I say hi, hello, or nod and smile. I use my inside voice to make thoughtful contributions. I look at people in the eyes. I listen to what they have to say, nodding to show that I understand. I ask questions or add to what they are saying. I stay focused on what we have been asked to do. When we finish, I thank them and give them a compliment.

An anchor chart as shown in figure 4.4 can help promote academic skills that some students may lack.

Figure 4.4

Sentence stems on an anchor chart help promote academic skills.

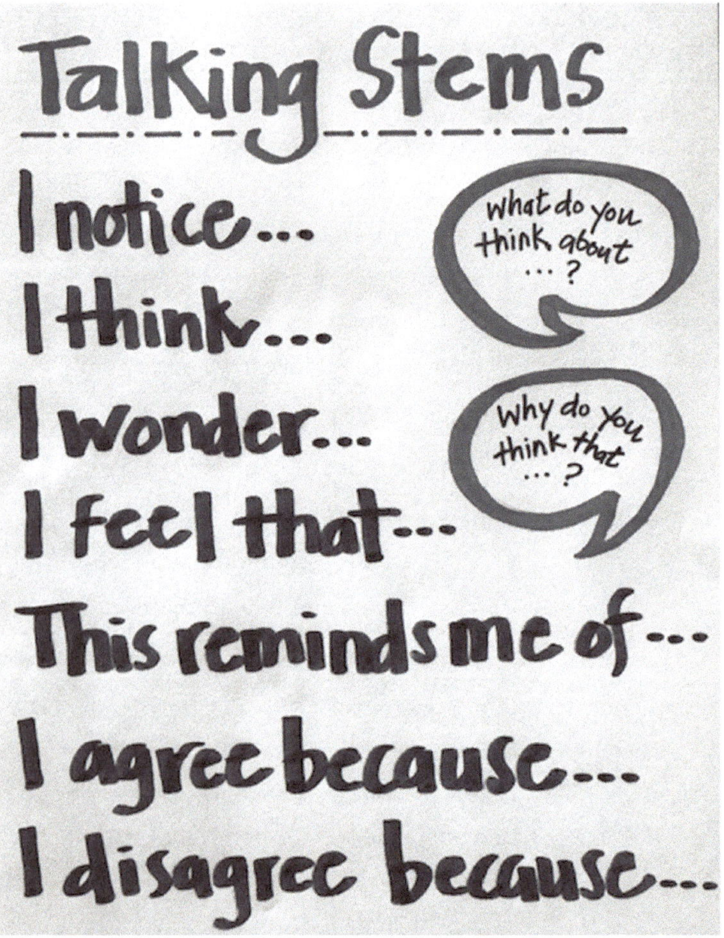

Teach Self-Regulation Skills

Not all students need explicit instruction in self-regulation skills, but for those who do, be ready for intervention on how they can manage their own behaviors. Research strongly supports that teaching students such skills increases their self-regulation competence that benefits the whole class (Busacca et al., 2015; McConnell & Synatschk, 2012). We define self-regulation as the application of the knowledge, skills, and attitude to improve one's own functional behavior or action, such as being able to recognize and manage emotions, calm down when angry, resolve conflicts respectfully, make responsible decisions, handle interpersonal situations effectively, and demonstrate empathy for others.

These skills involve instruction on self-monitoring emotions (*When I get angry, I want to scream*), social awareness (*If I scream, I disrupt the learning of others and that's not fair to them*), apply a technique to lessen the physical sensation (*I'll take a deep breath, and count to ten*), self-evaluation (*I did a nice job of taking a deep breath, looking around to see everyone working, and went back to work*), and self-reinforcement (*It worked. My classmates weren't upset with me. Great job!*). Some self-regulation skills to teach students who really need them, include:

- Describe physical sensations separately from emotions
- Identify and express emotions verbally
- Accept criticism and praise
- Take responsibility for actions
- Initiate a calming strategy after being upset
- Follow directions from adults
- Demonstrate empathy for others
- Identify consequences before acting
- Manage transitions
- Use adults for help when getting upset
- Act respectfully to others, regardless of differences
- Respect personal boundaries, rights, and property of others
- Negotiate with others when there is disagreement.
  (McConnell & Synatschk, 2012)

Students with emotional and behavior disorders who have 504 plans and IEPs often require the teaching of such self-regulation skills. When teaching these skills, use the strategies shown in figure 4.5 to enhance instruction.

Teach Calming Techniques

Consider teaching calming techniques to students to keep them from becoming too aroused and misbehaving. Such techniques can improve self-regulation and reduce psychological stress in children who practice it (Black & Fernando, 2014). These techniques involve deep breathing exercises and/or visualization practices. Deep breathing exercises include Belly Breathing, 4-4-4 Breathing, and Kiss Breathing (presented in figures 4.6a, 4.6b, and 4.6c), and visualization practices invite students to close their eyes, clear their minds, and imagine themselves having a fun time with loved ones (Campos & Fad, 2023). Additionally, they can collect and concentrate on pictures or images from the Internet that evoke calm (such as beaches or mountains) or they enjoy (such as superheroes, celebrities, or popular cartoon characters). Positive verbal statements can also boost students' self-confidence and improve their behavior.

Figure 4.5

Little Things That Work

 **Don't forget to . . .** use students' names when talking to them.	 **Remember to . . .** post their achievements and artwork around the classroom or hallways.	 **It doesn't take much to . . .** say, "Way to go," "You're amazing," or "I'm so glad you're in my classroom!"

Icon sources: Istock.com/bubaone; Istock.com/bgblue; and Istock.com/VectorCookies

Figure 4.6a

Belly Breathing

- Sit down on a chair or floor.
- Take a moment to relax your shoulders, arms, and legs. Shake these if it helps to loosen up.
- Place both hands on your belly.
- Close your eyes if you like.
- Breathe in through your nose and feel your stomach rise as the breath enters and your belly expands.
- Breathe out through your mouth.
- (In later breaths, the other hand can be placed over the chest).
- (Open your eyes after repeated practice).

Image source: Istock.com/Grace Elaine

Figure 4.6b

4-4-4 Breathing

- Choose to sit down on a chair or floor or stand.
- Take a moment to relax your shoulders, arms, and legs. Shake these if it helps to loosen up.
- Close your eyes if you like.
- Breathe in for a slow count of four.
- Hold for a count of four.
- Exhale for a slow count of four.
- Repeat.
- (Open your eyes after repeated practice).

Image source: Istock.com/nicoletaionescu

Figure 4.6c

Kiss Breathing

- Choose to sit down on a chair or floor or stand.
- Take a moment to relax your shoulders, arms, and legs. Shake these if it helps to loosen up your body.
- Close your eyes if you like.
- Inhale through your nose with your mouth closed for a count of 2.
- Exhale through your mouth for a count of 4 as you pucker your mouth like a kiss.
- Breathe out slowly.
- Repeat.
- (Open your eyes after repeated practice).

Image source: Istock.com/ Valentyna Melnyk

Pow! How? Now!	
POW!	What are your reactions to what you read so far?
HOW?	How will you use this information?
NOW!	What does this mean, especially with your most challenging students?

Icon source: Istock.com/nazarkru and Istock.com/lineartestpilot

PART III

INTERVENTION

SEVEN ESSENTIAL COMPONENTS OF BEHAVIOR INTERVENTION

CHAPTER 5

What's in This Chapter

- Seven Essential Components
  1. Use Your Attention and Relationship
  2. Signal, Warn, Restate Expectations
  3. Teach and Reteach
  4. Be Flexible: Change Activities, Resources, or Delivery
  5. Change the Environment
  6. Use Positive Reinforcement
  7. Provide Choices; Respect Individuality

Your Needs and Wants

I need to know more about your seven-component model before I even think about using any of the interventions. I want to know why I should follow your model.

Questions to Think About as You Read the Chapter

- How do you teach students to behave according to your expectations?
- How often do you alter your classroom to improve student behavior?
- How do you use positive reinforcement?

Interventions for changing student behaviors are everywhere. Teachers first learn about them in their pre-service college courses. They learn more about them in their professional development from presentations at conferences, their PLCs and RtI committees, teacher journals, postings on websites, and other sources. The challenge for many teachers is that they don't always know what interventions will work with *their* students. Just because one teacher uses an intervention and it works in their classroom, it doesn't mean it will work for another. To complicate matters, teachers rarely have time to research and design behavior interventions quickly and easily. With this in mind, we wanted to provide teachers with specific interventions for the top misbehaviors that they face in the classroom. As we mentioned in the Introduction, we used a model to guide us as we designed the fifty interventions. Here, you will learn about our seven-component model with reasons to support its use.

Seven Essential Components

We have discussed how important it is to use behavior interventions that are proven to have a positive impact. One way to know that is to review the evidence. Fortunately, education is a field in which research is carried out regularly and scholars publish their findings in journals, share them in conference proceedings, provide them as support for products and materials, and discuss them in online sites and forums. As we considered which of the many well-known behavior interventions to include in this book as interventions for the top ten misbehaviors, we reviewed that research. The body of evidence supports seven essential components that we identified as our guide (seen in figure 5.1) in designing the intervention.

Figure 5.1

Seven Essential Components of Behavior Intervention

7 Essential Components of Behavior Intervention	Use Your Attention and Relationship 	Signal, Warn, Restate Expectations 	Teach and Reteach 
Be Flexible: Change Activities, Resources, or Delivery	Change the Environment	Use Positive Reinforcement	Provide Choices; Respect Individuality

As many research articles indicated, typical behavior management systems include school-wide, classroom-based, and individual student-focused interventions, most of which should be preventative. Some specific interventions rise to the top and are mentioned frequently. Many of the "best practices" or "positive practices" in behavior management are identified and described in article after article by several authors. Readers who wish to explore some of the studies can find them in the references for this chapter.

For now, though, let's explore the seven components.

1. USE YOUR ATTENTION AND RELATIONSHIP

Being mentally present with students; Being physically nearby and focused on them; Meeting their wellness needs; Committing to strengthening bonds with them; Balancing instruction with appreciating their personality traits

We don't think of relationship building as an intervention. Rather, we see a basic requirement of good teaching. However, without the foundation of a positive student-teacher relationship, our seven essential components may not have as significant an impact as they would if teachers and students know, care, respect, and communicate with each other. This intervention is based on those relationships.

We presented this component first because it is effective and simple to use. Teachers already interact with students all day long and provide attention during most of the school day. There is no equipment needed and few, if any, materials required. Even though they are simple to use, they can be tricky. Too much attention for unwanted behaviors can inadvertently reinforce and increase them. Trusting a relationship too much might make the student think they can take advantage of your kindness and understanding.

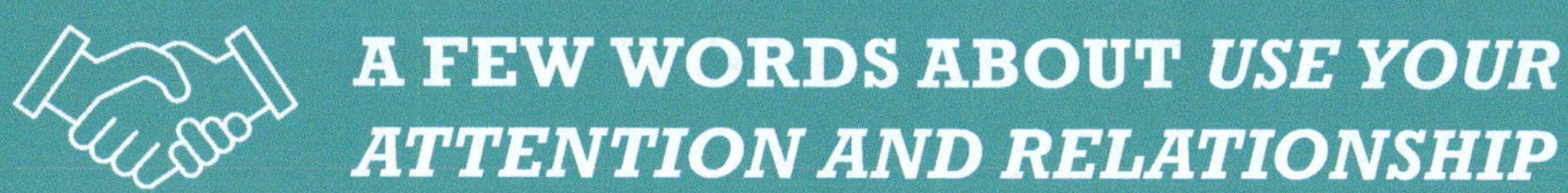

A FEW WORDS ABOUT *USE YOUR ATTENTION AND RELATIONSHIP*

- Focus on positive attention for positive behaviors rather than undue or counterproductive attention for misbehavior. When some students get teacher attention for behaviors that are not appropriate or prosocial, their behavior may get worse instead of better.
- Strengthen the student-teacher relationship by being consistent, building trust, and ensuring positive reactions to positive behavior. When students notice that teachers are consistently noticing their efforts, their trust in them and willingness to try often increase as well.

(Continued)

(Continued)

- Meet students where they are. Basic, visual, clear, and simple for some students; a bit more sophisticated for older or more complicated students. They recognize that while tangible positive reinforcers work very well for some students and are an important option, for many students, attention from a teacher matters more than other positive reinforcers.

2. SIGNAL, WARN, RESTATE EXPECTATIONS

Using cues as reminders; Using visuals or auditory signals; Reminding students of expectations and consequences

This component is so essential that when we reviewed the literature to determine which behavior interventions work best, this is at the top of the list. As an intervention, this does not require materials, a lot of preparation, or a complicated lesson plan. It can also be integrated into any teacher's instructional day. Many experienced teachers use this intervention often and with great success. The literature supports its effectiveness.

Signaling, warning, and restating are forms of communication. By adding these communication strategies to their repertoire, even the most effective teachers can improve the way they teach behaviors. Instead of constantly reacting to misbehaviors, using signals and warning students, often nonverbally, can accomplish more than a reprimand. Restating expectations is also an effective strategy. Think of it as presenting a math problem-solving strategy again and again. Even after you have presented it, practicing the strategy repeatedly with several examples and a variety of approaches is critical for student understanding.

A FEW WORDS ABOUT *SIGNAL, WARN, RESTATE EXPECTATIONS*

- Use cues without interrupting instruction. When a student is not meeting your expectations, make eye contact with the student and point to a poster or chart, tap/place a cue card on the student's desk, or restate your expectations (e.g., "I want you to clear off your desk and quietly line up when I call your name"). Build these into your management system so that they are not a random interruption.
- Cues teach behavior. Restating is a part of teaching. We do it for every subject and for almost every student. Think of it as clarification. We often clarify for others to be sure they understand.
- The cues keep the focus on expectations. This, as with the other interventions, emphasizes prosocial behaviors that teachers design (with student input), so they should be reasonable, age appropriate, and comfortable for both the teacher and the students.

3. TEACH AND RETEACH

Teaching prosocial behaviors that students have not learned; Not expecting positive behaviors but teaching them; Reteaching prosocial behaviors that students do not use consistently

Many teachers are shocked when they learn they have to teach behavior skills just like they teach academic skills. Fact is that many students come to school without some of the prosocial skills that we consider most basic. Unless teachers get to know a student, they may not realize which prosocial skills they know and which ones they don't. Some behaviors young children need that seem obvious, like sharing and listening, may not have been learned if the student never participated in play groups, preschool, or kindergarten. Older students might be expected to respond to constructive criticism or listen politely as someone gives them feedback, but those are high-level skills and many students have never learned them from an adult at home or at school.

Another issue for some teachers is that they have not been taught how to teach behaviors. Pre-service and in-service professional development is not all consistent, nor of high quality in all instances. Fortunately, we can still help teachers, even if it is not as in depth as some teachers need or want. The interventions that incorporate *Teach and Reteach* often recommend using a Looks Like/Sounds Like chart to explain what cooperation looks and sounds like or defining the steps a student can take as they learn to calm themselves.

A FEW WORDS ABOUT *TEACH AND RETEACH*

- The interventions using this component break down the teaching process into manageable steps. When teaching prosocial behaviors, this is important. For those teachers who lack background in how to teach positive behaviors, just knowing where to start can allay their fears and give them the confidence to begin the teaching process.
- Many of the interventions that incorporate *Teach and Reteach* target alternative or replacement behaviors. Even if teachers succeed at helping a student decrease a disruptive or dangerous behavior, that student must learn a new behavior to use instead. In other words, students need a positive and appropriate behavior to replace the misbehavior.
- *Teach and Reteach* focuses on prosocial behaviors that reflect the mental health of students. Specific behavioral issues in the classroom can be addressed with interventions that are sensitive to students' mental health needs.

4. BE FLEXIBLE: CHANGE ACTIVITIES, RESOURCES, OR DELIVERY

Varying instruction to keep students motivated; Using student interests and learning styles in activities; Maintaining consistent routines and procedures but adapting teaching methods to give students something to look forward to

It might seem contradictory to talk about flexibility in teaching after discussing the need for structure, consistency, and predictability in the classroom. Fortunately, the concepts are not at odds with each other. All classrooms need to be well organized—the physical environment, transitions, rules/expectations, procedures, management of materials, schedules, and paperwork. Teachers typically attend to these factors to ensure that their classes run smoothly. In chapter 2 we discussed ways in which behavior problems can be prevented, and organization and structure are the foundation of those strategies. Nevertheless, we suggest flexibility.

The main reason we suggest flexibility with activities, resources, and delivery of instruction is that each student is an individual. They are all different. To teach prosocial behaviors and then maintain them, teachers' interventions need to be flexible enough to change because students change. If a student comes to school on Tuesday morning after having an argument with his mom, missing breakfast, and forgetting his homework, the teacher's approach should be different from what happens on Friday, when the same student is on time, looking forward to the weekend, full from breakfast, and in a great mood. Little changes to activities, resources and materials, and the way that instruction or suggestions are delivered can make a big difference.

A FEW WORDS ABOUT *BE FLEXIBLE: CHANGE ACTIVITIES, RESOURCES, OR DELIVERY*

- Students come to school with lots of issues. Teachers have become more aware of significant mental health issues like depression and anxiety. Depression, especially, impacts mood. If students are not appropriately treated, including any necessary medications, their behaviors will require understanding and flexibility.
- Flexibility of activities, resources, and delivery of instruction is also a break from more authoritarian approaches (i.e., A "my way or the highway" attitude). The issue is not just that some students chafe under an authoritarian approach; the idea of forcing students to comply with directives is often not effective and it may escalate problematic situations.

- Changing the way that instruction or behavioral guidance is provided to students is respectful of student diversity and individuality. It is not realistic to expect teachers to individualize every lesson plan or activity. But if teachers fail to consider the differences in how students perceive, process, and express information, the time that *wasn't* spent in individualizing or accommodating differences will be consumed by dealing with student performance issues afterwards.

5. CHANGE THE ENVIRONMENT

Rearranging the classroom to meet the needs of individual and groups of students; Addressing movement, seating, materials, and so forth

Environmental changes to prevent or deal with misbehavior are one of the most frequently mentioned interventions for classroom misbehavior. We believe that there are several reasons for this. Environmental changes are easy to observe and measure, so researchers can easily determine if they have been implemented and, if so, whether any observable behaviors change. Environmental changes are also relatively easy for teachers to implement. Changing seating takes a little time, but it is not nearly as challenging as teaching a student to use a self-management technique to calm down when they are upset.

When changing the classroom environment, the sky is the limit. Teachers can change lighting, room arrangement for different activities (direct large group instruction, small groups, and individual learning), noise makers and noise levels, visual materials on the walls, partitions and shelves, teacher and assistant areas. They can also revamp computer storage and/or centers, book storage, student learning materials, instructional equipment like computers and whiteboards, and management tools. The environment can also include structures and procedures that the teacher uses to communicate about transitions; beginnings and ends; schedules for subjects, lessons, and activities; labels and containers at students' desks and tables; learning center boundaries and movement control signals; and many more factors.

A FEW WORDS ABOUT *CHANGE THE ENVIRONMENT*

- Changes to the classroom environment can also be individualized for students who have special needs. For example, if you have a student whose behavior escalates as they get distracted, using a simple environmental intervention like providing headphones might solve the behavior problem without significant time and effort.
- Environmental changes also have the advantage of destigmatizing interventions. Most students don't give a second thought to the teacher asking a student to set their personal timer at their desk. One day it might be their turn to use the timer and few students would consider that environmental intervention as embarrassing or different.

6. USE POSITIVE REINFORCEMENT

Using a consequence system with rewards for prosocial behaviors and/or meeting goals; Responding to positive, prosocial behaviors with descriptive praise; Having charts and menus that list privileges that students can earn

For teachers who have a background in behavioral studies, especially those related to precision teaching, interventions that use positive reinforcement to improve or change behavior should be easy to understand and easy to use. The simple definition teachers need to know is this: Positive reinforcement is any consequence that increases a behavior. This is important because something we *think* might be a positive reinforcer—since it increases *our* behavior—may only work for us, not for each and every one of our students. One student, for example, might enjoy the reward of drawing with the teacher's special markers and paper because he likes to draw. Another student might be disappointed with the same drawing "reward." Sometimes we provide incentives for students, but they do not increase positive behaviors because they are not desired and the behavior that precedes them does not change.

One way to find out if activities, tangible items, choices, and other available items to students will increase positive behaviors is to try them. The important thing to know about changing behavior is that if and when we find and use consequences students prefer, we can structure those consequences so that they follow desirable prosocial behaviors. Interventions based on positive reinforcement are appropriate for so many settings in a school environment—in hallways, outside at recess, in our classrooms, in the cafeteria, on the bus, while waiting for the bus, and during classroom lessons. Teachers who understand and use this tool are one step ahead.

A FEW WORDS ABOUT *USE POSITIVE REINFORCEMENT*

- Positive reinforcement is versatile. Teachers can use a wide variety of positive reinforcement options and vary them regularly so that they stay fresh and desirable. This allows teachers to individualize and reach those students who may be resistant to typical everyday consequences. For example, a student may not care about verbal praise, but responds positively if they get to sit at a designated "work by yourself" desk.
- Positive reinforcement can be simple. If a teacher decides to be purposeful and use specific praise after a student demonstrates a behavior, that may be all it takes to improve that student's behavior. Teachers may use more complicated positive reinforcement, but it may not be necessary for all students (e.g., have a store with currency the students earn for meeting her expectations).

7. PROVIDE CHOICES; RESPECT INDIVIDUALITY

Giving students choices and options; Letting students decide when and how to use their earned consequences; Allowing students choices about movement, seating, assignments, and so forth

The last essential component relates to providing choices for students and respecting their individuality. Some teachers might ask themselves, "What do choices have to do with behavior?" Providing choices and respecting individuality are foundational actions that all teachers should engage in all the time. These two actions are critical to establishing a positive culture in the classroom and emphasizing them for difficult behavioral issues can have a positive and lasting impact.

As teachers provide choices, they must balance fairness, equity, diversity, and individuality. When is it okay to give one student a choice but not another student? How many choices can a teacher manage in a busy classroom? Does individuality mean a different set of expectations for some students? These are challenging questions, and individual teachers may struggle to answer them. Our suggestion, specific to behavior in the classroom, is to remember that students come to school representing a wide range of experiences, prior support, nurturing, education, values, emotions, orientations, beliefs, religions, cultural expectations, health issues, abilities and disabilities, languages, expectations, fears, stressors, and other factors too numerous to mention. The student whose behaviors do not seem to make sense to their teachers can often be helped by building a strong teacher-student relationship, so the teacher knows them well enough to know what individual approaches will make a difference.

A FEW WORDS ABOUT *PROVIDE CHOICES; RESPECT INDIVIDUALITY*

- Research strongly supports that providing choices to students improves their behavior and academic engagement. Providing students with choices can transform them from apathetic learners to engaged and motivated learners.
- Respect for individuality gives students the knowledge that their teacher knows and respects them. They are seen, heard, and understood. For many upper elementary and middle school students, the feeling of being anonymous and invisible can be reduced or negated when teachers communicate an understanding of their individuality.

CLASSROOM CONNECTION

When you have a student who is reluctant to speak out in a large group or a student who is embarrassed that their English is not perfect and refuses to answer your questions, consider whether the issue is a cultural/linguistic difference or a behavioral issue. Talk to the student's family, consult with prior teachers, meet with your ESL/ELL specialist, or talk one-on-one with the student. You can easily use partner learning strategies instead of large groups, Yes/No answer cards, or individual dry erase boards instead of oral responding.

Pow! How? Now!	
	What are your reactions to what you read so far?
	How will you use this information?
	What does this mean, especially with your most challenging students?

Icon source: Istock.com/nazarkru and Istock.com/lineartestpilot

Readers who would like more information about research supporting these behavioral strategies can consult the chapter 5 references listed at the end of the book.

THE TOP TEN MISBEHAVIORS IN CLASSROOMS

CHAPTER 6

What's in This Chapter

- The Top Ten Misbehaviors
  1. Talking Out
  2. Moving Around/Leaving Seat
  3. Arriving Late/Delaying Start of Classwork
  4. Failing to Cooperate with Others
  5. Failing to Complete Assignments/Avoiding Work/Often Unorganized
  6. Refusing to Follow Directions
  7. Avoiding Social Interactions/Isolating Themselves
  8. Failing to Cope With Typical Classroom Expectations Because of Worries and Perfectionism
  9. Tantrumming to Get Their Way
  10. Violating Classroom Norms to the Point of Negatively Impacting Others
- Some Evidence Related to the Top Ten Misbehaviors

Your Needs and Wants

I need to know how you came up with the top ten. I want to know why you didn't address other misbehaviors that drive teachers crazy.

Questions to Think About as You Read the Chapter

- What are the top misbehaviors in your classroom?
- What specific misbehavior is most challenging?
- What interventions do you use with your most challenging misbehavior?

This chapter presents the top ten misbehaviors teachers are most likely to encounter in a classroom. The misbehaviors are presented as what students *do*, not what they do not do. To select the ten misbehaviors, we explored research-based articles, reviewed teacher resources we developed that addressed problematic behaviors, drew on our own experience as teachers, and consulted with other teachers. The top ten misbehaviors tend to lead to other problematic behaviors, interfere with teaching and learning, be recognized in the literature as disruptive, and have a ripple effect in the classroom (i.e., the behavior of one student impacts the behavior of other students). These misbehaviors also challenge the teacher's role as the leader in the classroom, and/or escalate to the point of being difficult to manage within the classroom. The bottom line: Misbehavior can have a serious negative impact on instruction, as well as students' emotional and mental well-being.

We did not include any aggressive behavior or other office referral offenses in the top ten list. School districts and the respective campuses typically have a list of office referral behaviors and response protocols for behaviors that are so serious that they are managed by the office or by personnel specifically assigned to deal with these serious offenses. These misbehaviors include illegal behavior, serious disruptions, unsafe behavior, behavior that is dangerous to others, weapons offenses, illegal substance possession, vandalism, leaving or entering school property when prohibited, abusive language, verbal and physical threats, and many other serious offenses. Our fifty interventions found in Part IV are not intended for any of those office-managed behaviors.

The Top Ten Misbehaviors

1. TALKING OUT

Talks out without permission, sometimes interrupting, bothering others, and making inappropriate comments

Many times, teachers are fine with students talking during a discussion if they are polite and respectful. However, when students talk out, interrupt others, or make inappropriate comments to the point that it interrupts instruction, disrupts others' learning, or causes social problems, it is important to intervene. Consistent talking out can make teaching almost impossible if talk outs are frequent. In addition, when some students make comments directed at other students, the talk outs not only disrupt teaching but they also disrupt the positive classroom environment and may prompt other students to respond, escalating the behavioral issues.

It is important to keep in mind that the goal is not a silent classroom; the goal is an appropriate level of conversation and comments that allow for socialization while making academic progress.

2. MOVING AROUND/LEAVING SEAT

Leaves seat or work area without permission

Most teachers are comfortable with movement in the classroom if that movement does not disrupt their teaching or students' learning or behavior.

However, when students leave their seats or work areas often, it is disruptive, especially when there is no need to be moving. Student movement in the classroom can impact instruction, learning, and classroom behavior. Some students bother others with comments or may touch other students and their materials. Other students who are seeking attention may take a long time for basic tasks like pencil sharpening, and draw out their out of seat time so that it is unreasonable and distracting.

Student movement is not the most serious of behavior problems, but it can have a domino effect and lead to other behavior problems. Fortunately, there are some reasonable, effective interventions that can help.

3. ARRIVING LATE/DELAYING START OF CLASSWORK

Is often tardy to school or slow to begin to work

When students are late to school, late to class, and/or slow to begin to do their schoolwork, their own learning is impacted, but instruction for other students is often negatively impacted as well. When tardiness (or delaying and failing to start a task) disrupts teachers' instruction and demands attention from the teacher or from students, it often takes time for teachers to repeat, redo, or provide individual attention. Reteaching, keeping track of late assignments, and scheduling makeup work are issues that take time away from instruction. Behavior problems may also occur when the student enters the classroom with excessive movement and talking.

A student's tardiness and delayed start to assignments may start as a low-level behavior, but it is one of the most annoying and disruptive. We understand that many districts and schools have policies related to tardiness that are nonnegotiable. Teachers must, of course, comply with district and campus policies. We are hopeful that our interventions do not conflict with required actions. Figure 6.1 provides little tips that help improve student classroom behavior.

Figure 6.1

Little Things That Work

 **Don't forget to** . . . ask parents/caregivers what works to keep their child focused or on task at home.	 **Remember to . . .** send home positive messages about each student.	 **It doesn't take much to** . . . send a text to parents/caregivers that says, "Your child is awesome!" with a photo of their achievement or artwork.

Icon sources: Istock.com/bubaone; Istock.com/bgblue; and Istock.com/VectorCookies

4. FAILING TO COOPERATE WITH OTHERS

Has difficulties working with others, cooperating in groups, and getting along

School is an important setting for teaching academic and social skills that help students succeed later in life. Apart from their homes, schools are the most positive and consistent social environments most students will experience. It is important that students learn to get along with others, relate to adults and other children and youth, and build lifelong skills like cooperating, communicating, and interacting effectively. These skills will help them succeed in the real world their entire lifetime.

Because classrooms are group situations and there are often small group structures for assignments, failing to cooperate with others can make a real difference in how much they learn and how they progress academically. Everyone has heard of the stereotypical student who is a brilliant loner and can learn everything on their own. While there are certainly some people who can learn independently, they are the exception, not the rule. When students do not get along with others, their academic achievement may suffer along with their socialization.

5. FAILING TO COMPLETE ASSIGNMENTS/AVOIDING WORK/OFTEN UNORGANIZED

Fails to complete assignments, especially independent work

There is an obvious relationship that teachers understand: Students who do more usually learn more. Conversely, students who fail to complete their assignments learn less than students who participate and do their work. Some assignments, like redundant homework or practice, may not result in increased learning, and teachers should be careful not to give assignments that are busy work. But when assignments are necessary, well designed, and relevant, students should complete them.

In addition to being critical for academic success, failure to complete assignments often leads to behavior problems as well. Students who are not working will often fill their time with other activities that can bother other students, disrupt instruction, violate classroom or school rules and expectations, and cause behavioral problems in class and/or in school. Completing work and doing what teachers assign is a win-win for students.

6. REFUSING TO FOLLOW DIRECTIONS

Refuses to follow classroom rules and procedures, including teacher directions and may argue when given directions

Refusals often occur in the classroom, where other students see and hear what is happening. These public refusals are often embarrassing and difficult for teachers, who sometimes struggle to maintain their authority and who find instruction difficult when challenged frequently.

Students who refuse to follow directions may also instigate arguments and escalate to verbal or physical aggression. These refusals can be seen as the first step toward aggression for some students. In addition to behavior problems in the classroom, refusals to comply with requests and directions also impacts students' academic success and social relationships. Academic achievement depends on students' demonstrating learning, and making and keeping friends often depends on being seen as a positive person. While there may be many reasons for the refusals, interventions are critical.

7. AVOIDING SOCIAL INTERACTIONS/ISOLATING THEMSELVES

Avoids interactions with others and is often not included or asked to join activities

Externalizing behaviors are behaviors that are directed outward and often bother others, disrupt instruction, threaten, or cause others harm, or are dangerous. These behaviors typically get a quick, strong reaction from school personnel, as they usually should. However, acting out behaviors are not the only problematic behaviors students today demonstrate.

When students demonstrate behaviors that are *not* acting out behaviors but instead are internalizing behaviors, it may seem like there is less incentive to respond because the behaviors may not be bothering others, disrupting instruction, or causing a disturbance. However, these internalizing behaviors, which can include fearfulness, withdrawal, and physical complaints, can be very serious and may result in long term harm to students. School is a social as well as academic environment, and it is helpful for teachers to know how to support and respond when students are withdrawn, isolated, or rejected by their peers.

CLASSROOM CONNECTION

One way to develop a classroom community where students feel they fit in is to help students develop positive attitudes toward everyone in the classroom, no matter their ability or cultural background. One teacher does this by using a strategy she calls, "Pass the Positivity Cone." At the start of the day, she decides on several positive behaviors, like greeting the teacher on arrival, having a cleared desk at the beginning of every lesson, and so forth. When she sees students who exemplifies them, she puts an orange cone on their desk that reads, "I'm amazing," "I have great ideas," "I do my best!" Throughout the day students pass the cone quietly to others when they see the behaviors in action.

(Continued)

(Continued)

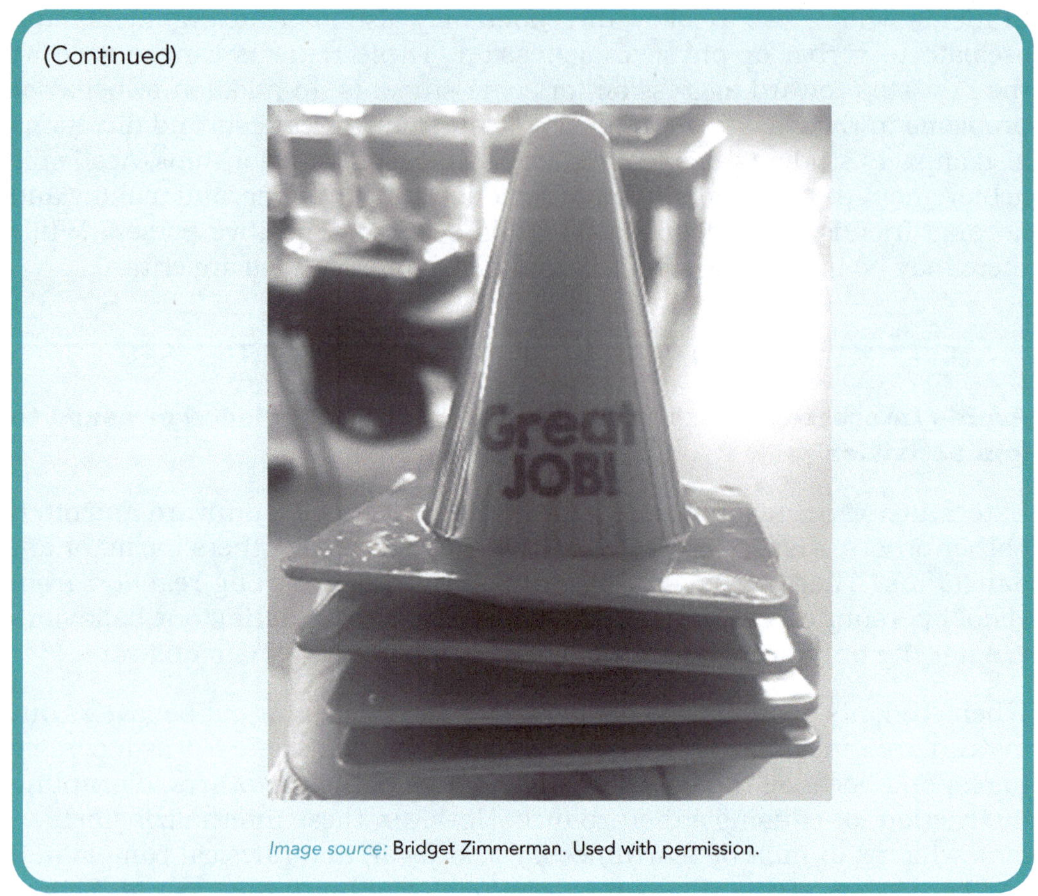

Image source: Bridget Zimmerman. Used with permission.

8. FAILING TO COPE WITH TYPICAL CLASSROOM EXPECTATIONS BECAUSE OF WORRIES AND PERFECTIONISM

The student has difficulty coping and expresses worries and fear of failure; may procrastinate or stop trying

Constant worrying, especially about what other people think, can be exhausting and emotionally draining. In today's world, when many students have access to social media and are bombarded with online content, worries are common. Students worry about how they look, what they said or didn't say, how they appear to others, whether they are missing out, and on and on. The toll on their mental health can be significant, including anxiety, depression, isolation, and sadness.

Students also worry in school about their academic work, again often comparing themselves to others or to unrealistic expectations. Students who tend to worry about performance, grades, the future may also be perfectionistic and rigid, always on edge and always anxious. The interventions we provide for worrying and perfectionism are intended for teachers, but students whose behaviors in these areas become extreme or interfere with their relationships and academic success may need a referral to a counselor or social worker.

9. TANTRUMMING TO GET THEIR WAY

Tantrums, cries, or yells when they don't get their way

Managing a busy classroom and providing effective instruction can be demanding and difficult. It takes time, effort, self-control, awareness, strength, and the ability to deal with several different issues at once. There is almost nothing that interrupts a teacher's management and instruction more than a student who loses control. Students can lose control physically (moving, throwing things, yelling), emotionally (becoming angry, crying, ignoring the environment), and certainly behaviorally (the added behaviors of threatening, cursing, blaming others, refusing to follow directions, and so on). A full-blown tantrum, whether demonstrated by a three-year-old or a twelve-year-old, can be disruptive, upsetting, and dangerous to both adults and children.

In our list of top ten behavior problems, we have differentiated tantrumming with crying and yelling from verbal aggression. While tantrums may include instances of verbal aggression, and some of the interventions are similarly effective, we view aggression as behavior intended specifically to threaten, frighten, or coerce someone. We suggest that while tantrum behavior may become aggressive, it originates from a loss of emotional regulation and involves an almost total breakdown of the student's self-control.

10. VIOLATING CLASSROOM NORMS TO THE POINT OF NEGATIVELY IMPACTING OTHERS

The student escalates their behavior to uncivil and/or threatening behavior

This is by far the most serious of the ten misbehaviors. Although we have included it and are providing interventions to help classroom teachers address this behavior pattern, this behavior can and should be referred to an administrator or other school official whose responsibilities include office disciplinary referrals, especially if the student escalates to cursing, yelling, or threatening. Teachers should never assume that they can safely manage a volatile student in a classroom setting where they and other students may be at risk for harm with special training and support. School districts typically provide specialized training to deal with defiance and refusals safely and nonviolently, and teachers should not be expected to intervene without that training when a student is displaying escalating behavior. Techniques that protect the student, the teacher, and other students are critical. Of course, any attempts to defuse a volatile situation should also follow district and campus policies and procedures.

Many times, even if all of cautions, suggestions, and guidelines suggested are followed and crisis prevention and intervention plans are in place, students who are noncompliant and are sent to other personnel for disciplinary action often return to the classroom. Sometimes, they are back in class quickly and with few additional supports. These students sometimes remain in the teacher's classroom long term. They are a cause for concern. The teacher will need effective interventions to address their behaviors.

As the teacher continues to teach the student, it is helpful for them to have tools to help teach the student alternative behaviors and ways to de-escalate. The interventions provided in this section are focused primarily on helping the student increase their awareness of their physical, emotional, and behavioral state and develop acceptable replacement behaviors. Teachers are always teaching and there are interventions to support teachers as they focus on these challenging behaviors. Counselors, social workers, behavior specialists, and others may also find these interventions effective.

Some Evidence Related to the Top Ten Misbehaviors

Those who wish to read more about classroom misbehaviors can consult the chapter 6 references listed at the end of this book. Several of the articles contain interesting and useful information that validates the misbehaviors we selected for intervention, as well as other evidence some educators may find useful. Some specific misbehaviors are noted for their frequency, others for their severity, and others for the impact that they have on instruction. Rather than get overwhelmed in trying to deal with what the articles mention are most problematic, we recommend that teachers instead focus on the misbehaviors that are an issue for their students in their classrooms, given their teaching style, skills, and overall management philosophy.

Pow! How? Now!	
POW!	What are your reactions to what you read so far?
HOW?	How will you use this information?
NOW!	What does this mean, especially with your most challenging students?

Icon source: Istock.com/nazarkru and Istock.com/lineartestpilot

PART IV

FIFTY INTERVENTIONS FOR THE TOP TEN MISBEHAVIORS

What's in This Part

- Directions for Using the Interventions
- Matrix: The Fifty Interventions and How They Incorporate the Seven Essential Components of Behavior Intervention
- The Fifty Interventions

Your Needs and Wants

I need practical interventions now! I want interventions I can use quickly and easily.

Questions to Think About as You Read the Chapter

- Which interventions will you use first?
- Which interventions will you use with individual students? Several students? The whole class?
- How will you track whether the intervention is working?

As listed in chapter 6, the top ten misbehaviors include:

1. Talking out
2. Moving around/leaving seat
3. Arriving late/delaying start of schoolwork
4. Failing to cooperate with others
5. Failing to complete assignments/avoiding work/often disorganized
6. Refusing to follow directions
7. Avoiding social interactions/isolating themselves
8. Failing to cope with typical classroom expectations because of worries and perfectionism
9. Tantrumming to get their way
10. Violating classroom norms to the point of negatively impacting others.

In this part of the book, you will find five interventions for each misbehavior for a total of fifty interventions.

●●● DIRECTIONS FOR USING THE INTERVENTIONS

Follow these directions for using the interventions to respond to the misbehaviors:

1. Look at the Matrix in figure 7.1 on page 87. You will see that the interventions are numbered from one to fifty. Each of the top ten misbehaviors has five interventions designed to address two or more of the seven essential components of behavior intervention (checkmarks indicate which of the seven components each intervention addresses). Then, evaluate whether the intervention is working. If it has had an impact on the misbehavior, continue using it. If not, select and implement another intervention for the same misbehavior. Change things up by using similar interventions if you think that what you are doing is getting stale or boring.
2. Consider pairing the selected interventions with other related misbehaviors. For example, a misbehavior for Failing to Complete Assignments might also be pertinent and useful for Failing to Follow Directions.
3. You can use more than one intervention at a time but be careful not to overwhelm yourself and the student by trying several interventions at once.

Figure 7.1 Matrix: The Fifty Interventions and How They Incorporate the Seven Essential Components of Behavior Intervention

		SEVEN ESSENTIAL COMPONENTS OF BEHAVIOR INTERVENTION						
		ATTN/ RELATIONSHIP	SIGNAL, WARN, RESTATE	TEACH/RETEACH	BE FLEXIBLE	CHANGE ENVIRONMENT	USE POS REINFORCEMENT	PROVIDE CHOICES
#	INTERVENTION							
	TALKING OUT							
1	Talk Tickets	✓	✓	✓				✓
2	Less Talk Signal Cards	✓	✓	✓			✓	
3	Attention Getters	✓	✓	✓	✓	✓		
4	Talking/No Talking	✓	✓	✓		✓	✓	
5	Nonverbal Signals				✓	✓		✓
	MOVING AROUND/ LEAVING SEAT							
6	No Need to Move			✓		✓		
7	Pick Your Place			✓	✓	✓		✓
8	Work Zones		✓	✓	✓	✓		✓
9	Body and Brain Breaks	✓			✓	✓		✓
10	Fidget Toys	✓	✓		✓	✓		✓
	ARRIVING LATE/DELAYING START OF CLASSWORK							
11	What's Going On?	✓			✓		✓	✓
12	Engaging Openers	✓	✓		✓	✓	✓	
13	Here's Your Spot	✓	✓			✓		
14	Help for Home	✓	✓	✓	✓	✓	✓	
15	On Time Tickets	✓					✓	✓
	FAILING TO COOPERATE WITH OTHERS							
16	Looks Like/Sounds Like		✓	✓	✓			
17	Encouragement Tickets			✓			✓	✓
18	How Am I Doing?	✓		✓			✓	✓
19	Group Listen		✓	✓			✓	✓
20	Double-Decker	✓	✓				✓	

(Continued)

(Continued)

	FAILING TO COMPLETE ASSIGNMENTS							
21	Cues Just for You		✓	✓	✓	✓		
22	Study Buddies			✓	✓		✓	✓
23	Finish the Puzzle	✓			✓		✓	✓
24	Head to the Quiet Zone		✓		✓	✓		✓
25	Timers Work		✓	✓	✓	✓		
	REFUSING TO FOLLOW DIRECTIONS							
26	How to Say It	✓	✓	✓	✓			
27	Good News/Bad News	✓		✓			✓	✓
28	What You Need		✓		✓	✓		
29	Ok Tickets	✓	✓		✓		✓	✓
30	Directions in Seven Steps		✓	✓	✓	✓		
	AVOIDING SOCIAL INTERACTIONS							
31	Check-in Chart with Talk Later Cards	✓	✓		✓			✓
32	Partner Do's		✓	✓	✓			✓
33	Everyone Is In				✓	✓	✓	✓
34	Time Tickets				✓		✓	✓
35	Inside/Outside Circles			✓	✓	✓		✓
	FAILING TO COPE WITH EXPECTATIONS BECAUSE OF WORRIES AND PERFECTIONISM							
36	My Worry Plan	✓		✓	✓	✓		✓
37	Worry Breaks		✓		✓	✓		✓
38	Visualize It		✓	✓		✓		✓
39	Reject and Replace		✓	✓	✓			
40	Personal Plan B	✓		✓	✓			✓
	TANTRUMMING TO GET THEIR WAY							
41	Just Say Thanks	✓	✓	✓				
42	It Pays to Say OK	✓		✓			✓	✓
43	Watch Yourself Stay Calm			✓			✓	✓
44	Say No Silently	✓	✓	✓	✓	✓		
45	After and Before	✓		✓				✓
	VIOLATING CLASSROOM NORMS TO THE POINT OF NEGATIVELY IMPACTING OTHERS							
46	A Plan to Go Along	✓		✓				✓
47	De-Stress	✓	✓	✓	✓	✓	✓	✓
48	Show Them Calm	✓	✓		✓	✓		
49	Do These Instead	✓	✓	✓	✓		✓	✓
50	Forgive and Move On	✓			✓			

INTERVENTION 1: TALK TICKETS

Misbehavior: Talking Out

Essential Components of Behavior Intervention Addressed

- Attention and relationship
- Signal, warn, restate
- Teach/reteach
- Provide choices

Need:

- Multiple copies of *Talk Tickets*
- A timer

Know:

Before beginning a discussion or question/answer session, decide how long you want the discussion to last. Take into consideration the age and attention span of your students and what kind of discussion it is (for example, explanation of new material, review of old material, generation of ideas, etc.). Review some behavioral skills, such as, "Only one person talks at a time," "Raise your hand," or "Wait for the last person to finish."

Do:

1. Copy and cut out the *Talk Tickets* from the reproducible, figure 7.2.
2. Give your talkative student (or all students) some tickets (e.g., one to two for a quick lesson; three to four for a longer one). These allow each student to talk a specific number of times.
3. Tell the students, "When you have a talk ticket available, you may talk. If you don't have a ticket left, you are done talking for this lesson."
4. Set the timer for the number of minutes you would like for the discussion.
5. When a student wants to make a comment, they hand you a ticket.
6. When their tickets are gone, their comments are finished. In addition to limiting the students who talk too much, if you use them with the whole class, you encourage the less talkative to use their tickets as well.
7. While you are limiting disruptive talk outs, make sure you allow for questions that clarify or explain the next activity.
8. Do not use this intervention indefinitely. Students' habits and behaviors should improve over time.

Figure 7.2 Talk Ticket

Image source: Istock.com/Evgeniya_Mokeeva

INTERVENTION 2: LESS TALK SIGNAL CARDS

Misbehavior: Talking Out

Essential Components of Behavior Intervention Addressed

- Attention and relationship
- Signal, warn, restate
- Teach/reteach
- Use positive reinforcement

Need:

- *Less Talk* Signal Cards

Know:

If students in your class have a problem with talking out regardless of the class or activity and generally talk too often, interrupt others, and disrupt your instruction, then re-explain your rules about talking, such as "Put away distracting materials," "Raise your hand and be recognized before talking," and "Make comments that add to the lesson." Review these rules regularly.

Do:

1. Review the rules for talking during a lesson. Do this quickly before beginning the lesson. The rules will vary depending on the age of students, the subject, the activity, and the purpose of the activity.
2. Remember that you are using nonverbal signals so that you are not providing extra attention for talking out, which may be exactly what the student is seeking.
3. Re-explain consequences that you have as part of your management system (positive as well as reductive/corrective).
4. Show the visual (figure 7.3) and display in a prominent area where students can easily see it.
5. Explain that you will point to (or tap) the signal to remind the student(s) that they need to stop talking.
6. Compliment students who are using self-control and talking out less.

Figure 7.3 Less Talk Signal Cards

Image sources: Istock.com/:Christian Horz and Istock.com/ lemono

INTERVENTION 3: ATTENTION GETTERS

Misbehavior: Talking Out

Essential Components of Behavior Intervention Addressed

- Attention and relationship
- Signal, warn, restate
- Teach/reteach
- Be flexible
- Change the environment

Need:

- *Attention Getters*
- Auditory signals (bells, chimes, or gongs) or visual signals

Know:

Explain your expectations related to attention and listening. A good example is to say that when you give directions or explanations, they need to do the following: Face the teacher; look at the board, book, or material being used; and, think about the lesson. Teach and review your expectations frequently. Use a bell, chime, or gong to let them know you are about to talk and they are to listen. You can also flash the lights off and on.

Do:

1. Before giving instructions or starting a lesson or discussion, wait for students' attention.
2. Use Attention Getters (figure 7.4) and look around to ensure that all students are paying attention. Don't be afraid to make up your own, based on your students' ages and interests.
3. After using the attention getter, give your instructions or explain the material, remembering not to talk so long that you lose students' attention.
4. Teach your students the *Attention Getter* routines and review them frequently.
5. Add new routines when you feel that students are losing interest.

Figure 7.4 Attention Getters

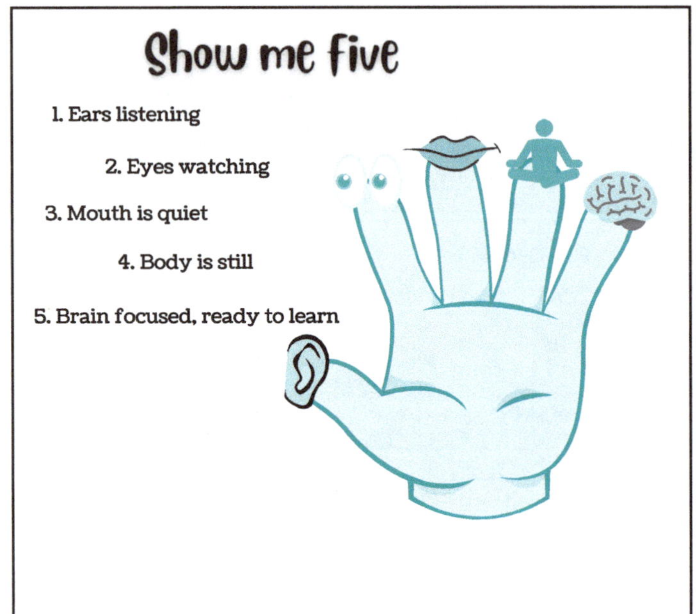

1-2-3 Eyes on Me

Repeat this phrase and then wait quietly and calmly for students to look at you and stop talking. You can also ask students to say the second phrase, "1 2 Eyes on You" to help them focus.

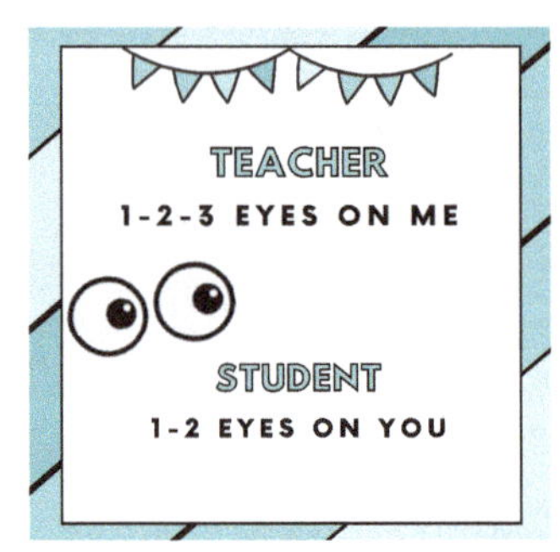

OTHER CALL OUTS	
THE TEACHER SAYS	**THE STUDENTS RESPOND**
All set?	You bet!
Ready to rock?	Ready to roll.
Hocus Pocus!	Ready to focus!
Zip it. Lock it.	Put it in your pocket.
Holy moly!	Guacamole!
Freeze. Everybody claps 3 times.	(3 claps)
Flat tire.	Shhhh
1 2	Listen and Do
Ready, set?	You bet!
Are you focused?	Yes, I am!

INTERVENTION 4: TALKING/NO TALKING

Misbehavior: Talking Out

Essential Components of Behavior Intervention Addressed

- Attention and relationship
- Signal, warn, restate
- Teach/reteach
- Change the environment
- Use positive reinforcement

Need:

- *Talking/No Talking* Sign
- Timer

Know:

As part of your classroom expectations, explain to your students that there are times in class when it is okay to talk and times when it is not okay to talk. Be specific and review these regularly.

Do:

1. Show students the *Talking/No Talking* sign (figure 7.5).
2. Discuss what the "Talking" sign means and what the "No Talking" symbol means.
3. Explain when each symbol will be used (e.g., "No Talking" when we take a test; "Talking" when we review for the test). Invite the students to offer other examples.
4. Model and practice with students and check to see if they can differentiate the expectations for each situation. Review as needed if you think that students are forgetting the expectations.
5. Start each lesson with a signal to get attention and then use a timer so that expectations related to talking are reasonable (e.g., five to eight minutes of no talking for young students; perhaps ten to twelve minutes for older students).
6. Alternatively, use a continuum of voice levels (such as figure 7.6) that encourages students to modify their volume, keeping in mind that there may still be times when students should not talk at all.

Figure 7.5 Talking/No Talking for Poster or Sign

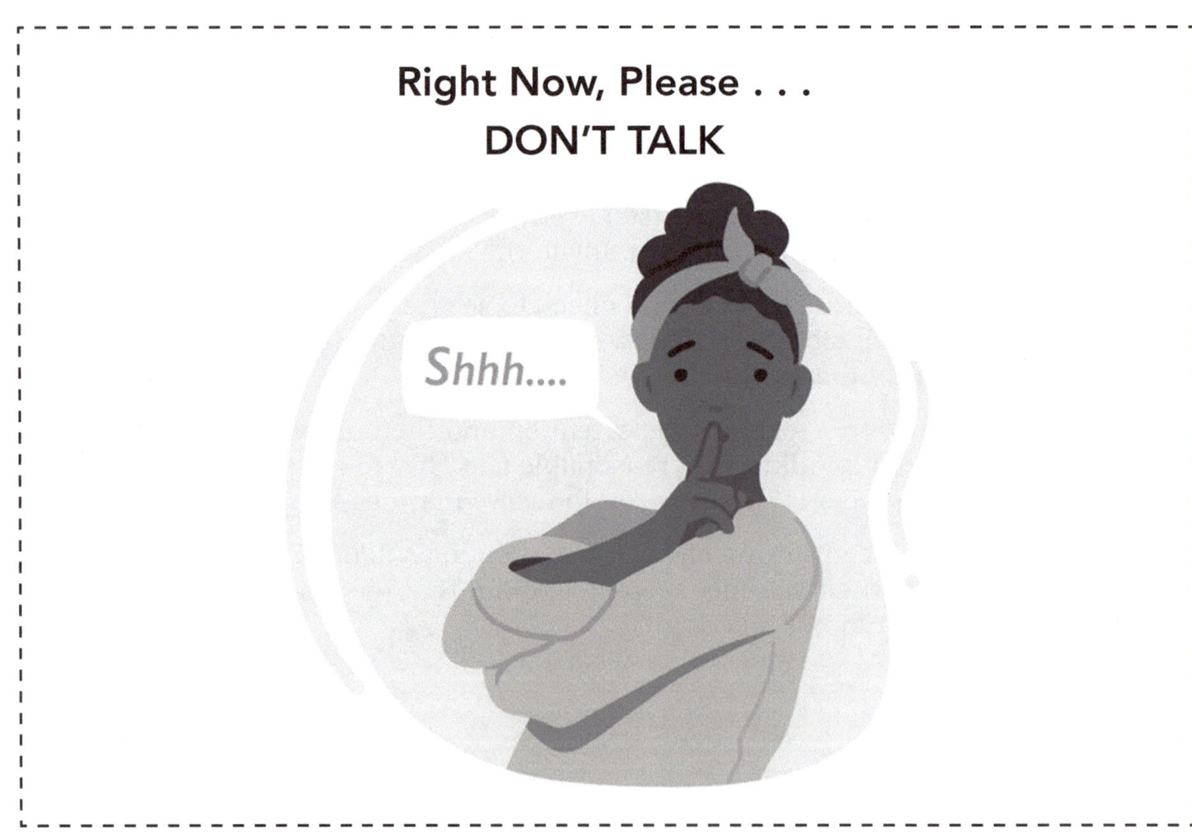

Image sources: Istock.com/ Colorfuel Studio and Istock.com/ lemono

Figure 7.6 Talking/No Talking Voice Levels for Poster or Sign

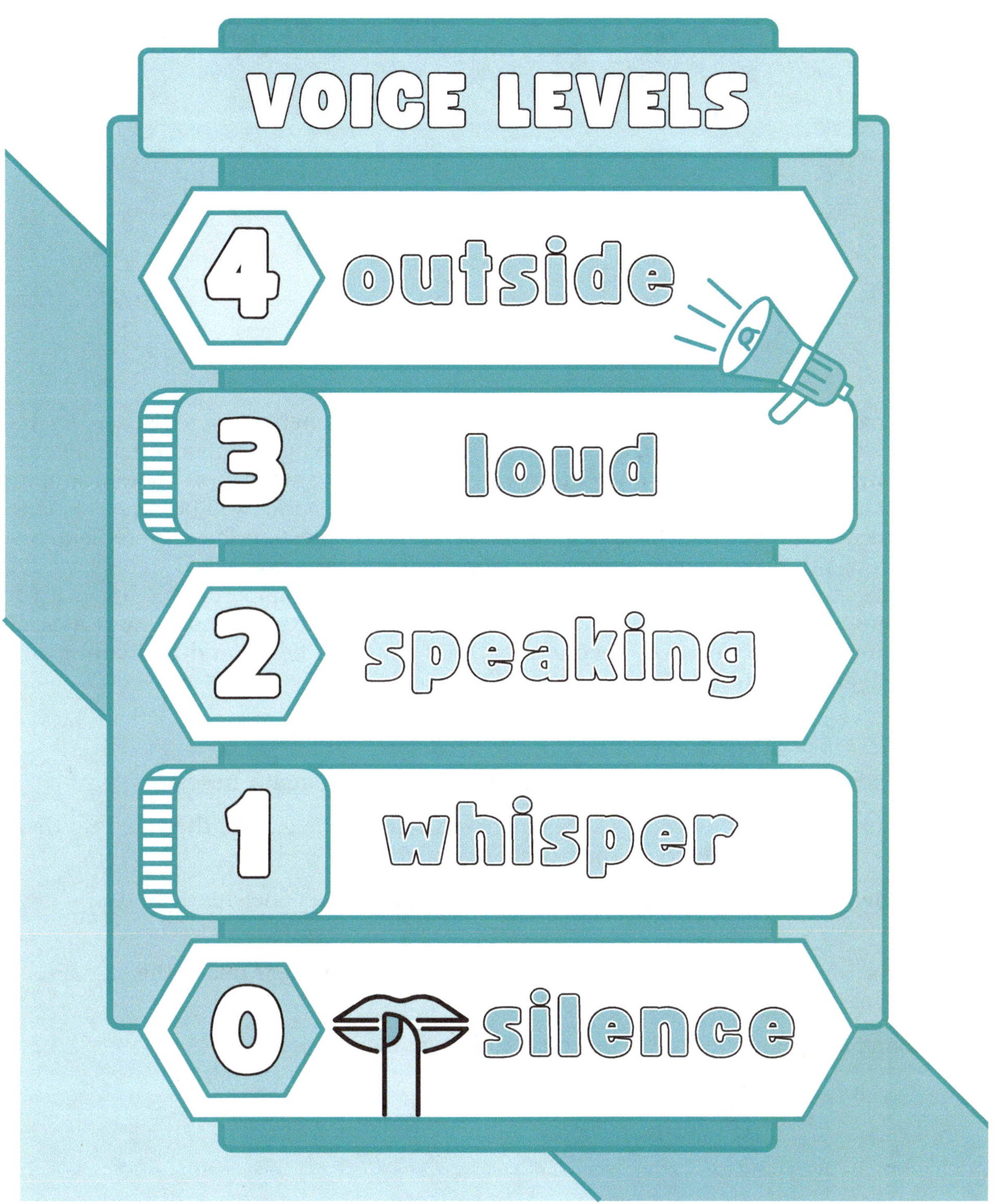

INTERVENTION 5: NONVERBAL SIGNALS

Misbehavior: Talking Out

Essential Components of Behavior Intervention Addressed

- Be flexible
- Change the environment

Need:

- Nonverbal signals

Know:

There may be times when students are working on assignments (not a discussion) and a student needs help or has a question. Those questions may be important, and ignoring them may frustrate the student and lead to other misbehaviors. There are many options available for nonverbal signals, and using them works well because students can indicate whether they need help, want to answer a question, have a problem, and other things they want to communicate. The most common nonverbal signals are finger or hand signs (e.g., raising your hand before talking, holding up one finger if you have an idea), but individual printed visuals are great for students to keep at their desks and use when needed. Keep in mind that simple is better and that young children will do best with one or two choices.

Do:

1. Decide on the signals (figure 7.7) that best fit your students' needs.
2. Teach the students how to use the nonverbal signals (e.g., Will they hold up their hand signal, put a card on their desk, or both?).
3. Model and role play when students use them, respond consistently and positively.
4. Set some ground rules with students so that you limit their use of the signals if necessary.
5. Explain what a reasonable response to a signal looks like.

Figure 7.7 Nonverbal Signals

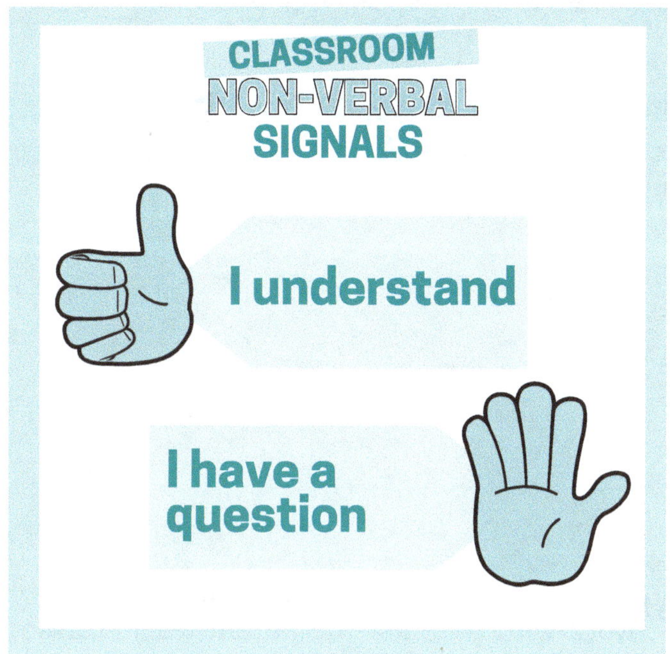

Source: Image adapted from istock.com/ SARMDY

INTERVENTION 6: NO NEED TO MOVE

Misbehavior: Talking Out/Leaving Seat

Essential Components of Behavior Intervention Addressed

- Teach/reteach
- Change the Environment

Need:

- Classroom Supplies
- Materials, Caddies, or Tubs

Know:

This strategy involves setting up the classroom environment to limit unnecessary movement. To minimize cost and loss, work with parents, the parent-teacher association, local stores, discount supply websites, and consider going to garage sales or asking local community organizations to help.

Do:

1. Arrange students' desks or tables so that supplies are available for every small group of students, which is about four students to a group.
2. Make sure that each group has a materials tub or caddies. An alternative is to use cardboard file boxes or leftover storage boxes from the school office.
3. In each caddy or tub, provide small individual pencil sharpeners, erasers, rulers, a box of tissues, extra sheets of paper, and any other supplies that students typically get out of their seats to find and access, as shown in figure 7.8.
4. There will still be many times when students can move freely in the classroom, but getting up to sharpen their pencil or throw trash away while distracting others will be limited.

Figure 7.8 Supply List for Easily Accessible Materials

SUPPLY LIST FOR EASILY ACCESSIBLE MATERIALS PLACE THESE SUPPLIES WHERE STUDENTS CAN ACCESS THEM *WITHOUT* LEAVING THEIR SEATS OR WORK AREAS.
1. Pencils
2. Pencil sharpeners
3. Erasers
4. Scissors
5. Paper
6. Small trash cans
7. Rulers
8. Markers
9. Glue
10. Tissues
11. Student water bottles
12. Calculators
13. Timers
14. Book marks/stick notes

Talking Out/ Leaving Seat

Example of Caddies

Image source: Istock.com/sleepyz

INTERVENTION 7: PICK YOUR PLACE

Misbehavior: Moving Around/Leaving Seat

Essential Components of Behavior Intervention Addressed

- Teach/reteach
- Be flexible
- Change the environment
- Provide choices

Need:

- *Pick Your Place* Chart

Know:

Giving students choices is often an effective way to prevent behavior issues in the classroom. With *Pick Your Place*, teachers allow students to choose where they want to work during certain class periods, lessons, or activities. Giving them this choice might remove their need to move around without permission.

Do:

1. Let students choose where to work from options you select (depending on the size of the classroom and the available space and the activity), such as:
   - A quiet place on the floor
   - Next to a friend
   - At a vacant desk or table
   - Standing in a place where no one else's view is blocked
   - In a beanbag chair or special piece of furniture
   - In the class library
2. When a class period or activity does not require students to sit in at their individual desks, show the *Pick Your Place* chart (on an electronic display or a poster-size version) and allow the students to move to their chosen workplaces. See figure 7.9 for examples.
3. If space is limited or too many students tend to select the same spaces, set a number ahead of time and use a random system to allow students to choose.

Figure 7.9 Pick Your Place

HERE ARE YOUR CHOICES FOR YOUR WORKPLACE CHOOSE ONE
☐ On the floor
☐ Next to a friend
☐ At a vacant table
☐ At your desk
☐ Standing
☐ At the class library
☐ In a special seat (bean bag chair, sofa, etc.)
☐ In a separate area with boundaries
☐ On a stability/balance ball
☐ On a stool
☐ Somewhere you can wear earphones
☐ Other: ______________________

Image source: Istock.com/ Nataliia Nesterenko

INTERVENTION 8: WORK ZONES

Misbehavior: Moving Around/Leaving Seat

Essential Components of Behavior Intervention Addressed

- Signal, warn, restate
- Teach/reteach
- Be flexible
- Change the environment
- Provide choices

Need:

- Colored Masking Tape
- Carpet Remnants or Small Rugs
- *Work Zones* Time Chart

Know:

Teaching students to recognize personal and group boundaries can be challenging, especially with young students and students who have disabilities related to sensory issues, hyperactivity, or visual impairments. However, when used sensitively and appropriately, the use of work zones with spatial boundaries is an excellent way to prevent behavior issues related to movement. Do not limit any student's movement to their work zone for extended periods of time, either daily or weekly, and do not use this strategy as a punishment or for the seclusion of any student.

Do:

1. Use colored masking tape to indicate borders for students' work zones. Use tape on the tables to indicate individual workspaces, and tape on the floor around desks or tables. Carpet remnants or small rugs can also show individual work zones.
2. Explain to your students that these are work zones.
3. Explain that these work zones are only in effect during certain times of the school day or for specific instruction. For example, if you are presenting a "direct teach" lesson and introducing new material, students should be in their work zone, listening and paying attention. However, if it is paired reading time, students may move and sit anywhere in the room with their partners.
4. When it is time to work in their zones, remind them of what type of work they are doing and why it is important to stay in their zone. Use the *Work Zone* Time chart (figure 7.10) to signal the students.
5. Set a timer so that you remember not to exceed the time limit.

Figure 7.10 Work Zones Time Chart

WORK ZONE TIME
Your teacher will signal when it's time to be at your work zone.
☐ When the teacher is about to explain something new
☐ When the teacher is about to give directions
☐ When you are going to work alone
☐ When you are going to read alone
☐ When it is quiet time
☐ When you need to take a quiz or test
☐ When you are working on something different from other students
☐ When you choose to work by yourself
☐ When you are working on an iPad or laptop and it may distract others

Image sources: Istock.com/poplasen and Istock.com/xavierarnau

INTERVENTION 9: BODY AND BRAIN BREAKS

Misbehavior: Moving Around/Leaving Seat

Essential Components of Behavior Intervention Addressed

- Attention and relationship
- Be flexible
- Change the environment
- Provide choices

Need:

- Videos, Games
- Body and Brain Breaks
- Access to Websites, Streaming Music, or Recordings

Know:

Schools can be stressful environments for students. Sitting quietly, paying attention, and working on academics require energy and sustained focus. Teachers typically expect students to do these things quietly and with little movement. The first step in this intervention is for teachers to acknowledge that students need to move throughout the day. Body and brain breaks are a great way to get them moving. Brain breaks also engage students in thinking, problem solving, and enjoyment that are not directly related to an academic subject. Body breaks are typically movement-based activities, including motor movements like exercises and games.

Do:

1. Decide when to integrate body and brain breaks into your daily schedule.
2. Refer to the *Body and Brain Breaks* reproducibles (on the next page) for some suggestions and build them into your schedule. For example, a five-minute midmorning break and a five-minute afternoon break will help students de-stress from academic expectations and build social relationships.
3. Explore these websites for additional ideas:

Figure 7.11 Website Links for Additional Break Ideas

ACTIVE SCHOOLS	PLAYWORKS	BE ACTIVE KIDS
https://www.activeschoolsus.org/	https://www.playworks.org/	http://www.beactivekids.org/

Moving Around/ Leaving Seat

Body and Brain Breaks

START WITH A SQUIGGLE; END WITH AN IDEA

1. Tell students they are going to be given a line drawing and they need to turn it into something else.
2. Draw a doodle on the board (e.g., a partial circle, a squiggly line).
3. Ask students to copy your doodle and add more lines to transform it into something else.
4. Have students share and explain what they drew.

REST AND RECHARGE

1. Set a timer for five to seven minutes.
2. Turn the lights down or off.
3. Play some calming background music. Streaming services can help you find spa music that works well.
4. Ask students to breathe in deeply for a count of four, hold their breath for a count of four, and then breathe out slowly to a count of four. Repeat twice.
5. Ask students to close their eyes and visualize something calm, such as ocean waves, clouds in the sky, colorful flowers, or the faces of people they love. They can put their heads on their desks as they start visualizing.
6. Toward the end of the set time, gradually increase the lights.

BALLOON BALL

1. Line students up in two lines, sitting in their chairs with the two lines facing each other. The two lines should be close enough to play the game, but not so close that they are touching (about two to three feet from each other).
2. The goal of the game is to hit the balloon over the heads of the other team. If they do, they get a point.
3. Students are not allowed to stand up or touch other students. They can lean forward or back to hit the balloon, but only one student at a time hits the balloon.
4. Toss the balloon into the air between the two lines.
5. Teams take turns hitting the balloon, one hit at a time per team.
6. Each time the balloon goes over the head of the opposing team and they can't reach it, a point is scored.

SCAVENGER HUNT

1. Give individuals students or pairs of students a list of five to ten items that are in the classroom and a time period to find as many of the objects as possible. See figure 7.12 for a sample chart to write in the items to be found.
2. Review the rules of the game: No grabbing from another student, no taking items from others' desks or backpacks, and no touching items on the teacher's desk. Use the appropriate voice/noise levels for this activity.
3. Set the timer for five to seven minutes. Students should find as many of the items as possible.
4. When the timer goes off, ask students to share what they found.

Figure 7.12 Scavenger Hunt

FIND THESE THINGS IN OUR CLASSROOM		

INTERVENTION 10: FIDGET TOYS

Misbehavior: Moving Around/Leaving Seat

Essential Components of Behavior Intervention Addressed

- Attention and relationship
- Signal, warn, restate
- Be flexible
- Change the environment
- Provide choices

Need:

- Fidget Toys for Individual Students (in bags/containers)
- *Fidget Toys* Signal Cards

Know:

For students who have problems sitting still or who move a lot in the classroom, gather a small collection of fidget toys and keep them in a bag or container. These can include stress and anxiety relief toys such as spinners, squeeze balls, pop bubbles, and slinkies. Also consider sensory Squishies and puzzle toys like the Rubik's Cube.

Do:

1. Collect a variety of fidget toys and explain your guidelines for using them to address noise levels, the timing of when and for how long students may use them, and how many students can use them at one time.
2. For students who have exceptional issues related to movement or sensory images, such as a student with ADHD or Autism Spectrum Disorder, design an individual plan for their use of fidget toys if using them seems to make a difference in their academics or socialization.
3. Give students a *Fidget Toys* signal card (figure 7.13) to make a nonverbal request, or you use the card to signal the students that they can use their fidget toys.

Figure 7.13 Fidget Toys Signal Cards

Image source: Istock.com/filo

Moving Around/ Leaving Seat

INTERVENTION 11: WHAT'S GOING ON?

Misbehavior: Arriving Late/Delaying Start of Classwork

Essential Components of Behavior Intervention Addressed

- Attention and relationship
- Be flexible
- Use positive reinforcement
- Provide choices

Need:

- *What's Going On?* Form

Know:

The purpose of this intervention is to determine why the student is chronically late. If you have built a relationship with the student, this conversation will go much easier. Keep in mind that there may be issues in the students' home and family that are making it difficult for them to get to school on time. Some of those circumstances may be embarrassing to the student. On the other hand, it could just be that the student is not highly motivated to come to school on time. You might want to keep track of your conversations with students who have intervention plans, 504 plans, or IEP's, and include dates, a description of interventions, and outcomes. Always respect the rules of confidentiality.

Do:

1. Find a time to meet privately with the student, even if it is only a conversation in the hallway or cafeteria.
2. Consult the *What's Going On?* questions (figure 7.14) you may want to ask the student. Use these as a guide to discuss with the student, not interrogate. Keep in mind that not all the questions are relevant or appropriate for every student.
3. Write down their information afterwards or just keep it in mind. You do not have to record the student's answers during the conversation.
4. Work to design an intervention with the counselor, RtI team, behavioral specialist, or social worker. If these personnel are not available in your school, follow up with the student and, when possible, a family member.

Figure 7.14 What's Going On? Form

USE THIS FORM AS A DISCUSSION GUIDE WITH THE STUDENT. YOU DO NOT HAVE TO ASK ALL THE QUESTIONS. SELECT A FEW THAT YOU ARE COMFORTABLE ASKING.

- I am interested in helping you do better in school. One thing that would make a difference is if you got to school/class on time. Let's talk about that.
- Can you tell me what's happening with you…what's making it difficult for you to get to school/my class on time?
- Is there anything you think I need to know about the problems you are having getting to school on time?
- Who can I talk to about helping you get to school on time? Can you give me a phone number?
- Would you be willing to talk to the counselor (or social worker, school psychologists, others)?
- Is there an adult here at school who you trust to help you? Who is that?
- What can I do? How can I support you so that you make it to school on time?
- Would you be willing to try some new ideas if I make some suggestions?
- What is one thing that would help you?
- What can you do to help yourself?
- Do you have a friend who could partner with you to help you get here?
- I am going to keep checking in with you. I care about you and am not giving up on you.

INTERVENTION 12: ENGAGING OPENERS

Misbehavior: Arriving Late/Delaying Start of Classwork

Essential Components of Behavior Intervention Addressed

- Be flexible
- Attention and relationship
- Signal, warn, restate
- Change the environment
- Use positive reinforcement

Need:

- Your daily schedule
- Prepared openers on the whiteboard, chalkboard, videos, or on paper

Know:

Students who are chronically late or tardy are not a uniform group. Some are late every day for no apparent reason, some are frequently late and may or may not have good reasons, and others are late just often enough to impact their learning and your classroom environment. Some students find school boring or irrelevant. This intervention aims to make the first activity of the day engaging and fun to counter negative attitudes the students may have about school.

Do:

1. As you build your schedule for the day or individual class period, take the time to design your first activity so that it meets at least one of these criteria:
   - It's interesting and engaging.
   - It's active and fun.
   - It sets the students up for success.
   - It provides an incentive (extra points, privileges, assistance).
   - It requires interaction, not passivity or solitary work.
   - It pre-teaches or reviews difficult material.
   - It's challenging.
2. Locate online and other resources and begin to create a library or collection of openers that fit the grade level, subject area, topics you are teaching.
3. Use the provided openers (on the next page) and others regularly and vary them. They can include brain teasers, body breaks, body and brain breaks, games, and extra credit or bonus activities.

Engaging Openers: Buzz, Create a Question . . . , Brain Teasers, and True or False

BUZZ

1. For young students, pick a number from 0 to 9. This is the "Buzz Number."
2. Students start to count off.
3. If the number they are supposed to say has the buzz number in it, they say "buzz" instead.
4. For example, the buzz number is 3, so students would say, "1-2-buzz-4-5-6-7-8-9-19-11-12-buzz."
5. For older students, step it up. You can use a number *and* all multiples of that number, so 3 and all multiples of 3: "1-2-buzz-4-5-buzz-7-8-buzz-10-11-buzz-buzz."

CREATE A QUESTION . . . AND ANSWER IT

1. Present the topic/subject of the lesson or class that is happening next.
2. Review three to five key words, rules, facts, names, formulas, or examples important to the lesson.
3. Ask students to work in groups of two to four and create one low level question (what, where, who question) and one high level question (how or why question).
4. Ask at least five groups to share their question.
5. Select several of the questions, write them on the whiteboard, and ask students from other groups to provide the answers to the questions orally.
6. Immediately after the discussion, choose five questions, ask students to write the answers, and count it as a quiz grade. This will give the habitually late student a little grade boost.

BRAIN TEASERS

Find books or online sources for these. Here are some examples:

- What five-letter word gets shorter when you add two letters to it? Answer: Short
- Can you add one mathematical symbol in between 55555 to equal 500? Answer: 555 – 55 = 500
- You are driving a bus. At the first stop, two women get on. Three men get on at the second stop, and one woman gets off. Two kids and their mom get on at the third stop, and four people get off. No one gets on at the fourth stop, and two people get off. You are at your final stop. What is the name of the bus driver? Answer: Yourself
- If you ran a race and passed the person in second place, what place would you be now? Answer: If you passed the person in second place, you'd be in 2nd place. You passed the person in second place, not first. You could only be in the first place if you passed the person who was in the first place before the race started.
- How many months have twenty-eight days? Answer: All twelve

TRUE OR FALSE? DECIDE. TELL THE TRUTH

1. Explain to students that as a review of what they have learned, you are going to ask them to determine if something is true or false.
2. Share five statements about what you are studying (e.g., novel, story, problem, strategy, experiment).
3. Ask students to tell you if each statement is true or false and explain their answer. Some questions can be obvious and some can be more challenging.
4. After the discussion, ask students to write one to three true statements about what they are learning.
5. Count this as a quiz grade. For the student who *always* needs a good grade to improve their average, this should encourage them.

INTERVENTION 13: HERE'S YOUR SPOT

Misbehavior: Arriving Late/Delaying Start of Classwork

Essential Components of Behavior Intervention Addressed

- Attention and relationship
- Signal, warn, restate
- Change the environment

Need:

- *Here's Your Spot* Place Cards

Know:

One of the biggest problems with students who are late to class is that they interrupt instruction. This can cause other students to lose their focus, interrupt teachers' instructional flow, and disrupt classroom behavior. One way to deal with this issue is to designate specific seats or areas for students who arrive late.

Do:

1. The seating areas/seats for students who are late should be near the door or at the back of the room, so that late students are less likely to bother other students or interrupt instruction.
2. Explain to everyone in the class that if they arrive late, they are to sit in the designated area when they enter the classroom. If you decide they can move to another seat later, let them know, but for the first several minutes, they need to stay in this area.
3. Use *Here's Your Spot* Place Cards (figure 7.15) to indicate where you would like them to sit.

Figure 7.15 Here's Your Spot Place Cards

Image source: Istock.com/owattaphotos

INTERVENTION 14: HELP FOR HOME

Misbehavior: Arriving Late/Delaying Start of Classwork

Essential Components of Behavior Intervention Addressed

- Attention and relationship
- Signal, warn, restate
- Teach/reteach
- Be flexible
- Change the environment
- Use positive reinforcement

Need:

- Contact Information for the Student's Parents/Caretakers
- Support from Other Personnel: Social Workers, Counselors, Home-School
- Liaisons, Community Members
- *Help for Home* Checklists

Know:

There are many reasons why students are chronically late to school or class and then slow to begin their classwork. Some students are late intentionally and have no interest in getting to class on time. Some others, though, may lack the needed supports at home to help them. Tardiness can have a serious impact on students' learning, so try these interventions and continue to seek solutions.

Do:

1. Communicate with parents and caregivers to see if they will allow help for the student. Follow your district policy for family outreach.
2. Students who are having problems getting to school or class on time may need some of these resources:
   - An alarm clock
   - A hook, a box, or space to put their backpack
   - Clothes and shoes
   - Hygiene products, such as soap, toothbrush and paste, hair brush
   - Simple meal-on-the-go foods like breakfast and protein bars
3. To raise funds, consider community resources, PTO/PTA special funds, local businesses or donors, and small mini-grants.
4. After gathering all the resources, find and follow your campus/district rules for home visits and, if possible, make a home visit to share the materials and explain how to use them. Students whose parents/families have approved of the resources can take them home on their own and use them immediately.
5. Review the checklists (figure 7.16) with the student using these directions: Use the *Night Before* checklist at home to get ready for school the night before. Use *Morning* checklist to get ready in the morning so you can be on time.

Figure 7.16 Help for Home

NIGHT BEFORE SCHOOL CHECKLIST
☐ My homework is finished
☐ My backpack has my books, homework, and papers that need to be signed
☐ I set my alarm
☐ I've picked out my clothes
☐ I put everything I need by the door

MORNING CHECKLIST
☐ Wash face and comb hair
☐ Eat breakfast
☐ Brush teeth
☐ Get dressed
☐ Double check backpack for books, homework, folders, and important papers
☐ Put on backpack

INTERVENTION 15: ON TIME TICKETS

Misbehavior: Arriving Late/Delaying Start of Classwork

Essential Components of Behavior Intervention Addressed

- Attention and relationship
- Use positive reinforcement
- Provide Choices

Need:

- *On Time* Tickets
- *On Time* Menu
- Items on the menu

Know:

Because it is always difficult to change habits, it is important to recognize and positively reinforce students when they are showing up for class on time and starting their work promptly. The *On Time Tickets* can be used for individual students or for all students. It is important to use them frequently and consistently enough so that they are effective.

Arriving Late/Delaying Start of Classwork

Do:

1. Use the *On Time* Menu (figure 7.17) or create one of your own with items that are age appropriate, inexpensive, and easy to provide. Consider "time with teacher" because many students enjoy the attention they get!
2. Give students tickets (figure 7.18) when they arrive on time to school or class. Be sure to pair the ticket with praise and a reminder of the items on the *On Time Menu.*
3. Allow students to redeem the tickets for the menu items.
4. Customize the menu to work with your students' ages and interests by using the blank boxes.

Figure 7.17 On Time Menu

ON TIME MENU	
YOU CAN EXCHANGE 5 TICKETS FOR	**YOU CAN EXCHANGE 10 TICKETS FOR**
Pick a song for the class to listen to today	Have a special lunch with the teacher
Visit the principal and share the good news	Pick a game for the class to play at indoor or outdoor recess
Line leader for the day	Call a loved one with the good news
Help pass out and pick up materials	Choose a buddy to work with
Lead the starter activity	Skip a homework assignment (teacher has to approve)

Arriving Late/Delaying Start of Classwork

Figure 7.18 On Time Tickets

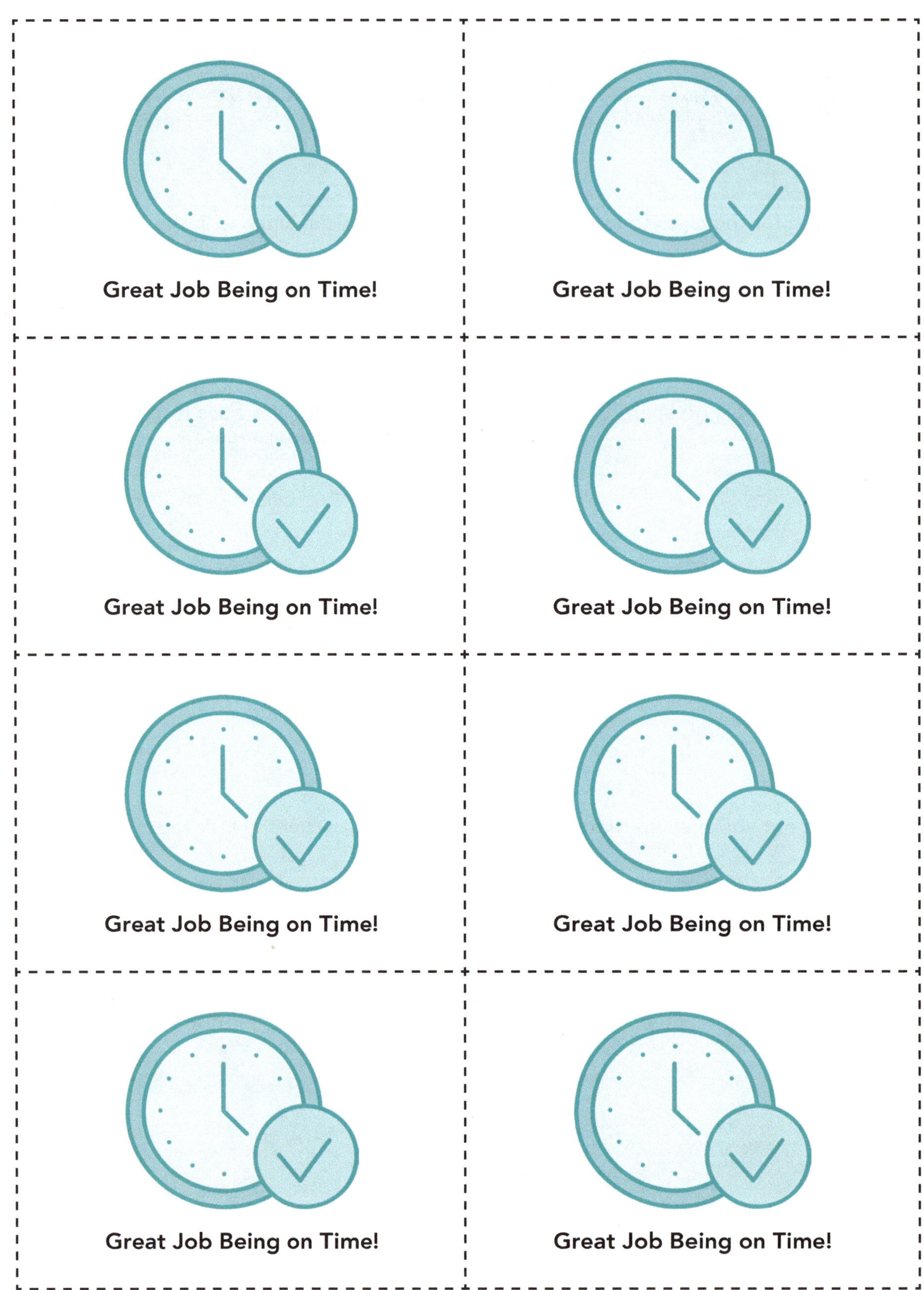

Image source: Istock.com/Drypsiak

Arriving Late/Delaying Start of Classwork

INTERVENTION 16: LOOKS LIKE/SOUNDS LIKE

Misbehavior: Failure to Cooperate With Others

Essential Components of Behavior Intervention Addressed

- Signal, warn, restate
- Teach/reteach
- Be flexible

Need:

- *Looks Like/Sounds Like* Chart (on poster, chart paper, or projected on screen)

Know:

Looks Like/Sounds Like charts are commonly used as tools for teaching social skills, including cooperating. One of the important characteristics of *Looks Like/Sounds Like* charts is that they can be used for all ages and grade levels and accommodate many learning styles and needs. Remember there is no one right answer to what cooperating in a group (or any other behavior) looks and sounds like in your class. It may change with different subjects, types of activities, or needs of your students. Some examples are provided after the blank reproducible.

Do:

1. Show students the blank *Looks Like/Sounds Like* (figure 7.19).
2. Discuss with students what you want to *hear* during group work and what you want to *see* during group work.
3. Focus on the word "cooperate" as you have this discussion and guide students to be very specific and clear about what cooperation means. For example, "Be nice" is not as clear as "Take turns talking" or "Compliment your partner."
4. Complete the chart with student input on what cooperating looks and sounds like, editing as you go along.
5. Review the *Looks Like/Sounds Like* chart when it is completed. Ask the students to provide specific examples of each and check with non-examples to make sure they are clear.
6. Review the *Looks Like/Sounds Like* examples for cooperation as shown in figure 7.20. Point out specific behaviors and ask students for input. Examples should meet your student's needs.

Figure 7.19 Looks Like/Sounds Like Chart

COOPERATING WITH OTHERS

Let's complete this chart before we do our group work. Tell me what you think we should see and hear when we work together in groups. I will add some ideas, too.

COOPERATING WHILE WE WORK IN GROUPS	
LOOKS LIKE	SOUNDS LIKE

Figure 7.20 Looks Like/Sounds Like Examples

COOPERATION	
LOOKS LIKE	**SOUNDS LIKE**
Taking Turns	"Please" and "Thank you"
Being Nice	"What do you think?"
Working Together	"I'm sorry."
Sharing Materials	"Can you help me?"

ROCKSTAR GROUP WORK	
LOOKS LIKE	**SOUNDS LIKE**
All eyes are on the task.	One voice is speaking at a time.
Everyone is sitting up or leaning in.	We are using a gentle tone of voice.
Group mates are facing one another.	Lots of questions are being asked.
One mouth moves at a time.	All voices get a turn.
Hands are busy with the task.	All voices get to finish their sentences.

INTERVENTION 17: ENCOURAGEMENT TICKETS

Misbehavior: Failure to Cooperate With Others

Essential Components of Behavior Intervention Addressed

- Teach/reteach
- Use positive reinforcement
- Provide choices

Need:

- *Encouragement Tickets*

Know:

To help teach and encourage your students to cooperate and work well together in groups, try using *Encouragement* tickets, which is a simple and easy-to-use tool. After the intervention, ask students to reflect on how they did with the tickets using questions, such as, How did you make positive comments using your tickets? Was your encouragement genuine? What did you do well? How could you improve?

Do:

1. Pass out tickets (figure 7.21) before group work. Each student should get about four tickets, adjusting for age and for the length of the discussion.
2. Explain that when working together in groups, it is important to encourage each other. If they don't know what the word "encouragement" means, explain, and make sure you add it to the *Looks Like/Sounds Like* chart (Intervention 16).
3. When a student does well and gets something correct, the students can say what's on their ticket to a team member and put it in the center of the table or on a pile in the middle of the group.
4. If a student tries but may not be one hundred percent correct, tell students to be encouraging and use the "Good try!" ticket and put it on the pile.
5. After the group work is over, discuss with students how it feels when others encourage them. Talk about how important positive behaviors are to people, even if they seem small.

Figure 7.21 Encouragement Tickets

Image source: Istock.com/calvindexter

Failure to Cooperate With Others

INTERVENTION 18: HOW AM I DOING?

Misbehavior: Failure to Cooperate With Others

Essential Components of Behavior Intervention Addressed

- Attention and relationship
- Teach/reteach
- Use positive reinforcement
- Provide choices

Need:

- *How Am I Doing?* Form

Know:

An important part of teaching is evaluating students' performance and providing feedback. It is also important that students learn to evaluate their own performance, especially when they are learning social skills and behaviors. For some students, group work is challenging, and it will take lots of practice for them to do well. Using this intervention requires that students self-evaluate and receive teacher feedback after each group work opportunity. These evaluations and the constructive ideas following them are part of teaching social behaviors. Comparing themselves to your expectations is a little reality check for some students who have difficulty reflecting on their own behavior.

Do:

1. Copy and pass out a *How Am I Doing?* Form (figure 7.22) to each student.
2. Review the expectations for group work using the *Looks Like/Sounds Like* Chart (Intervention 16).
3. Ask them to self-evaluate their behavior in the group after the group activity. They rate how they did and how they think *you* think they did.
4. Have private conversations with students who need support in group cooperation and/or students who are making great progress and deserve praise.

Figure 7.22 How Am I Doing? Form

In group work, I am trying to get better at (Circle the skills you are working on):

1. Listening to Others
2. Taking Turns
3. Making Positive Comments
4. Staying With the Group
5. Sharing
6. ______________________________

How I think I'm doing:	1 poor	2 unsatisfactory	3 satisfactory	4 very satisfactory	5 outstanding
How my teacher thinks I'm doing:	1 poor	2 unsatisfactory	3 satisfactory	4 very satisfactory	5 outstanding

In group work, I am trying to get better at (Circle the skills you are working on):

1. Listening to Others
2. Taking Turns
3. Making Positive Comments
4. Staying With the Group
5. Sharing
6. ______________________________

How I think I'm doing:	1 excellent	2 good	3 medium	4 poor	5 very bad
How my teacher thinks I'm doing:	1 excellent	2 good	3 medium	4 poor	5 very bad

INTERVENTION 19: GROUP LISTEN

Misbehavior: Failure to Cooperate With Others

Essential Components of Behavior Intervention Addressed

- Signal, warn, restate
- Teach/reteach
- Use positive reinforcement
- Provide choices

Need:

- *Group Listen* Card

Know:

Some students are naturals in group activities. They listen, take turns, share, contribute, and are polite and respectful. But other students lack these skills and talk nonstop, don't talk at all, or interrupt all the time. To help students have a positive group experience, pair this intervention with *Looks Like/Sounds Like* (Intervention 16) and focus on listening.

Do:

1. Explain how listening is a basic skill to use when working in groups.
2. Give each student one *Group Listen* card (figure 7.23) laminated for durability.
3. Remind them of good listening skills by reviewing the statements:
   - Sit up straight and face the person who is talking.
   - Make eye contact.
   - Smile or keep face relaxed, nodding occasionally.
   - If you have something to say, tell the group or raise your finger or hand.
   - Use "Way to go!" or "Good try!" phrases after someone else offers an idea. See Intervention 17 for other encouraging phrases the students can use.
4. Model the skill using the statement on the card.
5. Practice the skills regularly.

Figure 7.23 Group Listen Card

BE A GOOD LISTENER IN YOUR GROUP

Sit up straight. Face the speaker.

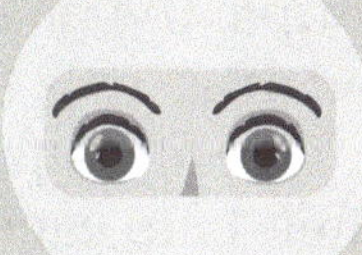

Make eye contact.

Smile OR just relax your face.

Signal if you want to talk.

Say "Way to go!" or "Good try!"

INTERVENTION 20: DOUBLE-DECKER

Misbehavior: Failure to Cooperate With Others

Essential Components of Behavior Intervention Addressed

- Attention and relationship
- Signal, warn, and restate
- Use positive reinforcement

Need:

- *Double-Decker* Cards

Know:

When students are learning to cooperate with each other in groups, the teacher cannot be everywhere at once to remind, prompt, and compliment students. This intervention is a great way for students to cue and compliment each other. The cards provide them with the language and ideas to use as they learn to work together, help each other, and encourage the whole group.

Do:

1. Copy and cut the reproducible (figure 7.24) to create two decks of cards, Group Social Skills and Teamwork Skills. If you wish, copy each deck in separate colors.
2. Instruct the students to shuffle the cards and place them in the center of the table in the two decks.
3. Before beginning the group work, each student takes one card from each deck, reads it silently, and places it in front of them.
4. As the group work proceeds, each student should say the phrase or sentence or perform the action on each card when it is appropriate.
5. After repeating or doing what is on the card, they can put the card at the bottom of the deck.
6. If needed, the teacher can remind students to refer to their cards and/or draw additional cards if it is a long activity.
7. Circulate throughout the room and take note of the students who did especially well.
8. Do a quick check and ask students how they felt about the *Double-Decker* Cards. Then reinforce students and call attention to the noticeable attempts that students made. Repeat specific comments that students made and compliment their efforts.

Figure 7.24 Double-Decker Cards

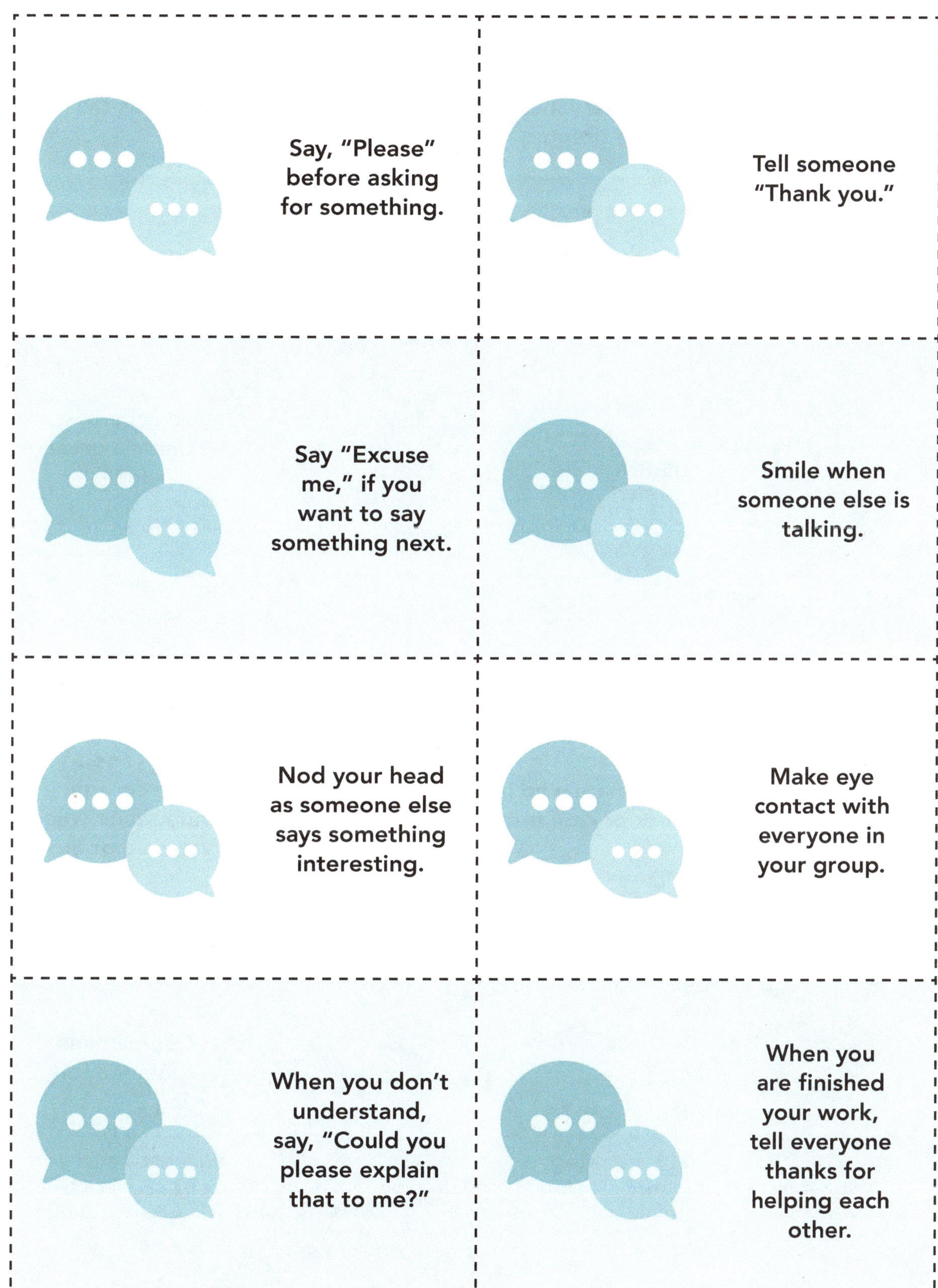

Image source: Istock.com/irem soyler

Failure to Cooperate With Others

TEAMWORK Share materials with everyone in the group.	TEAMWORK Take turns talking.
TEAMWORK Tell a team member you appreciate their hard work.	TEAMWORK Tell someone, "That's a great idea!"
TEAMWORK Offer to help a teammate who is stuck or confused.	TEAMWORK Check in with everyone to make sure they understand what you said or did.
TEAMWORK Ask the group for more ideas or for a strategy.	TEAMWORK Compliment someone for trying their best. You can say, "That was hard and you really tried. Great try!"

Image source: Istock.com/LvNL

INTERVENTION 21: CUES JUST FOR YOU

Misbehavior: Failing to Complete Assignments

Essential Components of Behavior Intervention Addressed

- Signal, warn, restate
- Teach/reteach
- Be flexible
- Change the environment

Need:

- *Cues Just for You* Cards

Know:

Directions and signals are important for all students in the class to see and respond to, but some students often need individualized reminders. However, talking to some students individually may draw them further off task or give them attention that makes the problem worse. Use the *Cues Just for You* Cards when the class is completing an assignment, but one or two students are off task, doing something nonproductive, or not working at all.

Do:

1. Tell the students that sometimes you will communicate with them nonverbally and that when you do, you want them to respond to your direction or request and do so without talking out loud.
2. Have the cue cards (figure 7.25) accessible during instruction.
3. Place a card on the student's desk when they are off task.
4. Point to the card.
5. Tap on it lightly.
6. Establish eye contact with the student.
7. Move away and give them a chance to refocus on their work.
8. If the student still doesn't get busy, privately remind them of incentives, remind them of consequences, and warn them.
9. Collect the cue cards and start fresh after a lesson or class.

Figure 7.25 Cues Just for You Cards

Image sources: Istock.com/Armation74; Adapted from istock.com/ bankrx; Istock.com/ trigubova; Istock.com/Shendart

INTERVENTION 22: STUDY BUDDIES

Misbehavior: Failure to Complete Assignments

Essential Components of Behavior Intervention Addressed

- Teach/reteach
- Be flexible
- Use positive reinforcement
- Provide choices

Need:

- *Study Buddies* Cards

Know:

Students often do not complete assignments because they can't remember the assignment, can't find their materials, or are just so unorganized it is difficult for them to do their work. They often need help with organization, but busy teachers do not always have the time to help them. Teaching students to help each other is a great way to provide support while continuing instruction in the classroom.

Do:

1. Each week assign students to pairs as study buddies. Do this thoughtfully and vary your assignments.
2. Copy and laminate the *Study Buddies* Cards (figure 7.26) so that each student has one.
3. Before the start of the day or lesson, give each student a *Study Buddies* Card.
4. Ask students to put their name and their buddy's name on the card. Set the timer for three minutes (give or take, depending on your students' ages) and have them check supplies and homework. Be clear about what supplies are needed and what the homework was. Put a tally mark on the tally sheet next to each Buddy pair that does their check.
5. In the afternoon, ask students to do a *Study Buddies* check of homework assignments and books/papers that need to go home. Again, give them a tally mark for completion.
6. At the end of the week, provide incentives for study buddies who completed their cards each day and helped keep each other on track.

Figure 7.26 Study Buddies Cards

STUDY BUDDIES

Date: ____________

Name: ____________________

Name: ____________________

❶ MORNING – I checked my buddy's:

☐ Supplies ☐ Homework

❷ AFTERNOON – I made sure my buddy had:

☐ Assignments ☐ Books and Papers

STUDY BUDDIES

Date: ____________

Name: ____________________

Name: ____________________

❶ MORNING – I checked my buddy's:

❷ AFTERNOON – I made sure my buddy had:

STUDY BUDDIES

Date: ____________

Name: ____________________

Name: ____________________

❶ MORNING – I checked my buddy's:

☐ Supplies ☐ Homework

❷ AFTERNOON – I made sure my buddy had:

☐ Assignments ☐ Books and Papers

STUDY BUDDIES

Date: ____________

Name: ____________________

Name: ____________________

❶ MORNING – I checked my buddy's:

❷ AFTERNOON – I made sure my buddy had:

Source: *From Practical Ideas That Really Work for Students With Autism Spectrum Disorders: High Functioning Autism* (p. 108), by Kathleen McConnell and Gail R. Ryser, 2014, Austin, TX: PRO-ED. Copyright 2014 by PROED, Inc. Reprinted with permission.

Here Are Some Things Buddies Can Do

1. Help each student practice memorization of math facts, spelling words. and vocabulary definitions.
2. Check to see if their buddies have necessary books, paper, and a pencil for class.
3. Quiz each other with flash cards.
4. Check to see if their buddies have written down the assignment.
5. Make sure their buddies put homework assignments and materials in their backpacks.
6. Ask each other to state or restate key points of a lesson.
7. Edit each other's written work.
8. Compare answers and then correct mistakes.
9. Practice oral assignments like poetry recitation, science experiment results, book reports, or explanations of the steps in math problems.

Source: *From Practical Ideas That Really Work for Students With Autism Spectrum Disorders: High Functioning Autism* (p. 108), by Kathleen McConnell and Gail R. Ryser, 2014, Austin, TX: PRO-ED. Copyright 2014 by PROED, Inc. Reprinted with permission

INTERVENTION 23: FINISH THE PUZZLE

Misbehavior: Failing to Complete Assignments

Essential Components of Behavior Intervention Addressed

- Attention and relationship
- Be flexible
- Use positive reinforcement
- Provide choices

Need:

- Puzzle with four, six, nine, or twelve pieces (consider student age and attention span)

Know:

When students are not in the habit of completing assignments, sometimes they need a boost. Using positive reinforcement is often effective for many students, and it helps if the reinforcement is student-selected and visual. In this intervention, the students work toward completing a puzzle of a selected activity or object, which becomes their reward.

Do:

1. Take a picture of something the student really likes or enjoys, such as extra computer time, skipping a homework assignment, or having lunch with the teacher.
2. Print the picture and cut it into pieces. Keep the number of pieces low (four to six) for young children. Consider more pieces for older students.
3. Each time the student completes an assignment, they earn a piece of the puzzle. Place the puzzle on their desk or on a nearby shelf if it's too distracting.
4. Reward the students with the selected activity or object after all the pieces have been earned and the puzzle is complete.
5. Use the blank reproducible (figure 7.27) and glue a photo or draw/write on it.

Figure 7.27 Finish the Puzzle

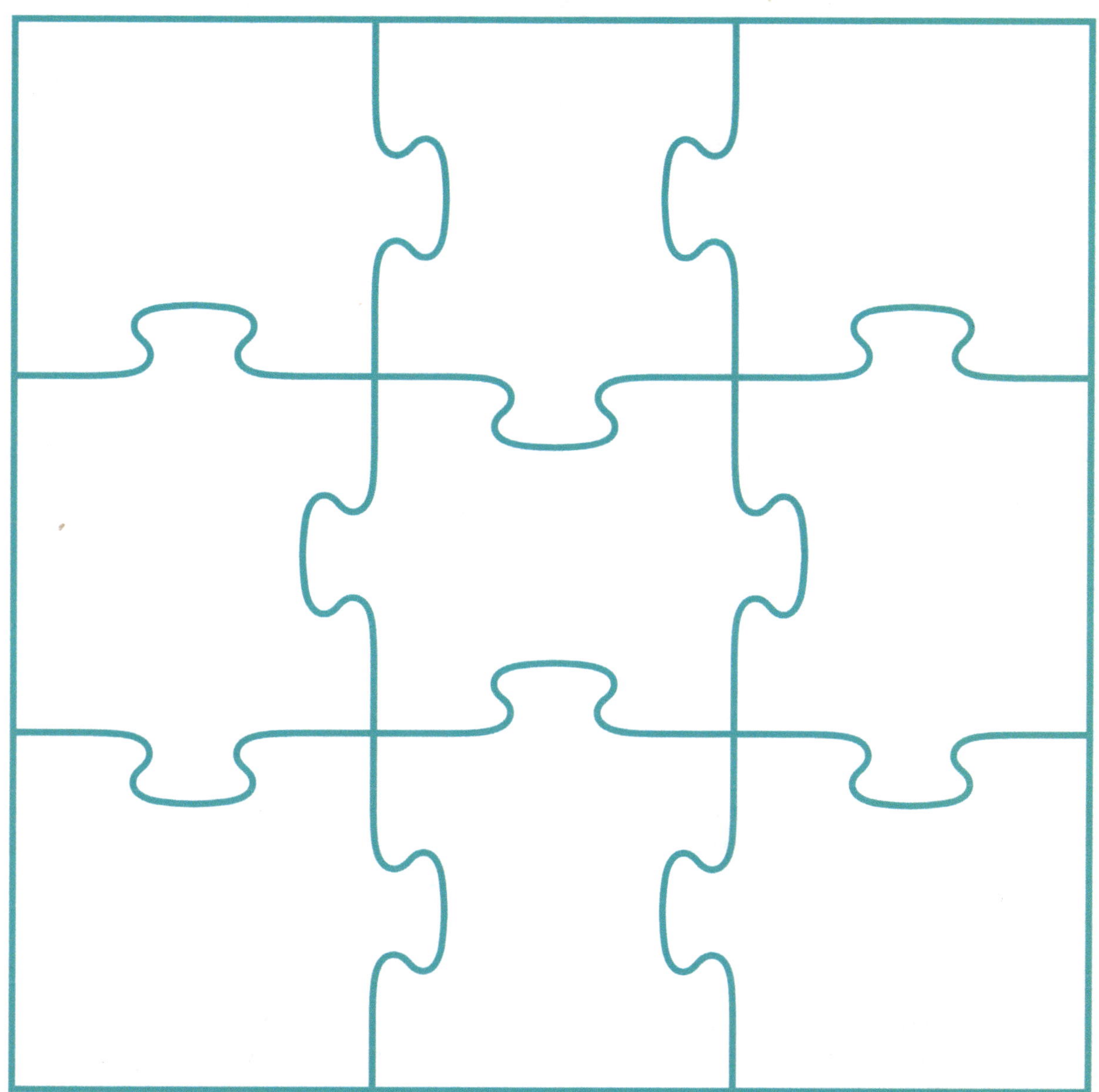

Image source: Istock.com/Iryna Sklepovych

INTERVENTION 24: HEAD TO THE QUIET ZONE

Misbehavior: Failing to Complete Assignments

Essential Components of Behavior Intervention Addressed

- Signal, warn, restate
- Be flexible
- Change the environment
- Provide choices

Need:

- *Head to the Quiet Zone* Cards
- A desk or area in the classroom that is quiet
- Headphones or ear buds

Know:

Some students are easily distracted by movement, noise, light, smells, or other sensory stimuli. For those students, work completion can be difficult because they have problems sustaining their focus. Consider creating a quiet zone in your classroom and supplying it with headphones that cancel out distracting noises. Use the *Head to the Quiet Zone* Cards to ask the student to move to the quiet zone or for the student to request to move on their own. The quiet zone should not be overused or used as punishment.

Do:

1. Set up a quiet zone and supply it with headphones, perhaps a boundary (like a cardboard divider on the desk), and anything else you think will help your distractible students.
2. Copy the *Head to the Zone* Cards (figure 7.28) and explain to students how they will be used.
3. Hand them a *Head to the Quiet Zone* Card when you can tell that a student needs a less distractible environment. If a student knows that they are distracted and need to move to concentrate, they can hand you a *Head to the Quiet Zone* Card and, with your permission, move to the quiet zone.
4. Set a timer for a reasonable amount of time to finish the assignment.
5. Ask them to return to the group space when the time is up.

Figure 7.28 Head to the Quiet Zone Cards

Image source: Istock.com/Roman Kybus

INTERVENTION 25: TIMERS WORK

Misbehavior: Failing to Complete Assignments

Essential Components of Behavior Intervention Addressed

- Signal, warn, restate
- Teach/reteach
- Be flexible
- Change the environment

Need:

- Various Timers

Know:

Using timers in the classroom helps support many students who need some structure, especially when they are working independently. Timers are great because they reduce teacher talking and take some of the challenge away from students/teachers (You are not telling them; the timer is!). There are many different types of timers, such as visual, class size, individual, stopwatches, and sand timers. Have several on hand and use them as needed, keeping in mind that there may be some students with disabilities who will not do well with specific types of timers or some conditions for using them. Individualize as needed. Using timers consistently so that they become part of the structure of the class will help routines and expectations remain consistent.

Do:

1. Set the timer for assignments, clean up or organization moments, and getting ready to work.
2. Use an individual quiet timer for students who need visuals directly in front of them.
3. Play incentive games with the timer, such as, "I bet you can't line up quietly in two minutes. But if you can, you get two extra minutes of recess."
4. Use a visual timer during tests or quizzes, so students know how much time they have but you don't interrupt them.
5. Play Beat the Clock by challenging students with, "Can you beat the clock and ____ in less than three minutes?"
6. See the *Timers Work Chart* (figure 7.29) for times you can integrate the use of timers as supports for students.

Figure 7.29 Timers Work

HERE ARE MOMENTS WHEN YOU CAN INTEGRATE THE USE OF TIMERS AS A SUPPORT FOR STUDENTS.
☐ For individual student's work completion.
☐ To streamline getting ready to transition.
☐ To pass out or clean up materials.
☐ As a limit on talking.
☐ To get students seated after they enter the room.
☐ To cut down on talking during quiet time like independent reading or test taking.
☐ In games.
☐ When you provide rewards to students.
☐ To cue students on computers or other devices.
☐ As a reminder to you not to talk too long.

INTERVENTION 26: HOW TO SAY IT

Misbehavior: Refusing to Follow Directions

Refusing to Follow Directions

Essential Components of Behavior Intervention Addressed

- Attention and relationship
- Signal, warn, restate
- Teach/reteach
- Be flexible

Need:

- *How to Say It* Cards

Know:

This intervention provides three brief, simple scripts for how to give directions to students who typically do not follow directions. However, it is important to make sure that before beginning to use these, you are ready to use Interventions twenty-seven, twenty-eight, twenty-nine, and thirty. In addition, review your system of consequences and be ready to use them. Recognize that the key feature these three scripts have in common is that in each, the teacher does not repeat the direction endlessly, argue with the student, threaten the student, yell at the student, or lose composure. It is difficult to stay calm, but essential.

Do:

1. Use the *How to Say It* Cards (figure 7.30), which are strategies called Speak and Spin, Please/Now, and Please Do It Anyway.
2. Review the three *How to Say It* strategies. Always keep a card with each prompt accessible. Refer to them often.
3. Practice with a strategy. If it doesn't fit your needs, try another.
4. Get as consistent as you can with the student who doesn't follow directions.
5. Give some time for each to work.

Figure 7.30 How to Say It Cards

SPEAK AND SPIN

1. **After giving a direction to the whole class,** move closer to the student who has not followed your direction.

2. **Stand close** (one to three feet away) and quietly use the student's name and then repeat the direction (e.g., "Eric, please begin the math review sheet.")

3. **Immediately after giving the direction,** turn and move away and do not give the student any further attention at that moment. Do NOT engage further with the student.

4. **After giving the student two to three minutes to begin,** repeat Step two above, then again turn and move away. If the student begins, reinforce them immediately (e.g., "Thank you for starting your work quietly" or "Ooh, I can't wait to see what you write").

5. **If the student still does not follow directions,** have your system of consequences ready.

*Note that this is a quick interaction to give the student an opportunity to do what you have asked. You are not ignoring a student who needs help.

PLEASE/NOW

1. For the student who typically does not follow directions, use a scripted set of directions.

2. Move about two to three feet away from the student and start your direction with the word "Please." Use a firm, strong voice, but do not raise your voice to the point that other students hear and notice you.

3. Make sure you give a one-step direction. Don't ask the student to do two or three things; just one.

4. Look at the clock or your watch and give the student one minute to begin. Do not stand over the student; move to help another student or look at someone else's work.

5. If the student does not begin within the one-minute time period, give the direction a second time. Begin this direction with the word, "Now," (e.g., "Now put your name on your paper.") Use a firmer voice, but do not yell.

6. If the student still does not begin, explain the consequences that are in place and then move away.

Refusing to Follow Directions

I KNOW. PLEASE DO IT ANYWAY.

1. This strategy is especially helpful for those students who have excuses and arguments ready for every direction you give.
2. After you give a student the direction, sometimes they will immediately begin to respond with refusals (e.g., "This is too hard." "I hate this." "This is stupid." "I can't do this." "This isn't fair." And so on. . . .)
3. Look at the student calmly and say these two sentences, "I know. Please do it anyway."
4. If the student continues to offer refusals, repeat your sentences, "I know. Please do it anyway."
5. Repeat the sentences up to three times, then move away.
6. Your consequences should be in place and ready to go.

INTERVENTION 27: GOOD NEWS/BAD NEWS

Misbehavior: Refusing to Follow Directions

Essential Components of Behavior Intervention Addressed

- Attention and relationship
- Teach/reteach
- Use positive reinforcement
- Provide choices

Need:

- *Good News/Bad News* Chart

Know:

Intervention 26, *How to Say It*, recommends three ways that teachers can address students who do not follow directions. These are great communication strategies. However, none of them will work long term without follow through. In this intervention, you and the students outline the consequences for following directions. Pair this with a *Looks Like/Sounds* Like chart (see Intervention 16) to explain what you mean by following directions.

Do:

1. Project the *Good News/Bad News* Chart (figure 7.31) on a poster board or whiteboard.
2. Work with students to write the positive and reductive consequences on the *Good News/Bad News* chart. Ask students to say what they think should happen if they follow directions, and what will happen if they don't.
3. Review the chart daily so that students understand.
4. Follow through with the consequences on the *Good News/Bad News* chart. Revise and reteach as needed.
5. Be consistent with the implementation.

Refusing to Follow Directions

Figure 7.31 Good News/Bad News

FOLLOWING DIRECTIONS	
THE GOOD NEWS: IF YOU *DO* FOLLOW DIRECTIONS, YOU EARN . . .	THE BAD NEWS: IF YOU *DON'T* FOLLOW DIRECTIONS, YOU WILL . . .

FOLLOW DIRECTIONS EXAMPLE	
THE GOOD NEWS: IF YOU *DO* FOLLOW DIRECTIONS, YOU EARN . . .	**THE BAD NEWS: IF YOU *DON'T* FOLLOW DIRECTIONS, YOU WILL . . .**
A High Five! Smiles All Around	Get a reminder to *Follow Directions* (and finish your work)
Tickets for the "I Did It" Drawing	Not earn "I Did It" tickets
A note or phone call to home	Prompt the teacher to let your family know you need to follow teacher directions.
The right to learn more, and your grades will improve	Probably fall behind and the classwork will be more difficult. Talk about that with your teacher.
Class privileges like line leader, official "complimenter"	Meet with the teacher at the beginning of recess to talk about doing the work you refused to do. Make a plan to get it done.

INTERVENTION 28: WHAT YOU NEED

Misbehavior: Refusing to Follow Directions

Refusing to Follow Directions

Essential Components of Behavior Intervention Addressed

- Signal, warn, restate
- Be flexible
- Change the environment

Need:

- *What You Need* list of the materials students need for the next class or lesson
- *What You Need* sign for outside the door or for students' tables or desks

Know:

There are many reasons why students refuse to follow directions. One assumption is that some students do not follow directions, especially for academic work, because they are not ready. Not being ready can include not having the necessary materials. If a lack of materials is the problem, using a *What You Need* list can help students respond to your directions. To increase the likelihood they follow directions, you want them to know what they need as they enter the classroom.

Do:

1. List the materials needed for the next class or lesson on the whiteboard or a poster. See the *What You Need* List example in figure 7.32.
2. Display the list outside the door (or give students their own copies) if students need to get materials from their cubbies, lockers, or desks.
3. Ask them to have the items on the list and be ready to follow teacher directions.
4. Place the list on group tables or desks, as an alternative, so that students can gather their materials and be ready for instruction without a lot of talk from the teacher.

Figure 7.32 What You Need List Example

WHAT YOU NEED
For the next lesson, bring:
☐ Pencil or pen
☐ Crayons
☐ Markers or colored pencils
☐ Highlighters
☐ Scissors
☐ Paper
☐ Glue
☐ Ruler
☐ Tablet/iPad/laptop
☐ __________ book
☐ Library book
☐ Interactive notebook
☐ Planner
☐ Workbook
☐ Calculator
☐ ______________________________
☐ ______________________________

INTERVENTION 29: OK TICKETS

Misbehavior: Refusing to Follow Directions

Refusing to Follow Directions

Essential Components of Behavior Intervention Addressed

- Attention and relationship
- Signal, warn, restate
- Be flexible
- Use positive reinforcement
- Provide choices

Need:

- *OK Tickets*
- *OK Menu*
- Small baggie for students to store their *OK Tickets*

Know:

It is always a good idea to have a variety of approaches for intervening when students need support for good behavior. *OK Tickets* are an easy-to-use positive reinforcer, and they also serve as a reminder for the student of what they *should* be doing.

Do:

1. Have a supply of *OK Tickets* (figure 7.33) in your pocket or hand before you start to give a behavior direction ("Please line up for lunch") or academic direction ("Please start reading on page 322").
2. Give each student who followed the direction quickly and without arguing an *OK* ticket (immediately after giving the direction). No comments are needed except praise for the students who followed your direction.
3. Allow students to trade in their *OK Tickets* for something on the *OK Menu* (figure 7.34) once or twice a week. Tailor the example so that it has items of high interest and value to your students.
4. As they select something from the menu, remind them that you appreciate it when they say, "Okay" and follow your directions.

Figure 7.33 OK Tickets

Image source: Istock.com/Vladimir Ivankin

Refusing to Follow Directions

Figure 7.34 OK Menu

OK MENU	
Trade in Your OK Tickets for These Items	
Sit in the Cool Seat	_____ tickets
First in the lunch line	_____ tickets
Extra headphone time	_____ tickets
Pick your own classroom job	_____ tickets
Read with a buddy	_____ tickets
Call a loved one and brag	_____ tickets
Tell the class a joke	_____ tickets
Messenger for the day	_____tickets
Bring something for show and tell	_____tickets
Bring stuffed animal to school	_____tickets
Lunch with your favorite adult	_____tickets

INTERVENTION 30: DIRECTIONS IN SEVEN STEPS

Misbehavior: Refusing to Follow Directions

Essential Components of Behavior Intervention Addressed

- Signal, warn, restate
- Teach/reteach
- Be flexible
- Change the environment

Need:

- The *Directions in Seven Steps* Script

Know:

Teachers eventually develop their own routine for giving directions. But first, try a highly structured sequence to get comfortable with a routine. *Directions in Seven Steps* builds in some checks to make sure that the student(s) understand the direction and can restate them. Before starting to give directions, always make sure students have the needed materials. Then be ready to signal students to give you their attention. By using a structured sequence like the script provided, you are teaching students a routine that they will become comfortable with and follow through with each time.

Do:

1. Use the *Directions in Seven Steps* script (figure 7.35) to explain and teach the sequence.
   - Get the students' attention.
   - Say the directions. Keep these simple.
   - Make sure that students understand the directions by asking what the directions are.
   - Repeat the directions.
   - Ask students to repeat the directions to a buddy.
   - Wait seven seconds.
   - Signal the start with "You may begin."
2. Complete the sequence calmly, not too fast, or too slow. The sequence should take less than a minute.

Figure 7.35 Directions in Seven Steps Script

1. Please give me your attention. Thank you.

2. Here's the direction. Please ____________________. (Give the direction.)

3. What is the direction? Please repeat the direction.
(Students repeat the direction.)

4. Again, here's the direction. Please ____________________.
(Give the direction again.)

5. What is the direction? Please repeat the direction to your neighbor/partner.
(Students repeat the direction.)

6. I am giving you seven seconds to start (choose the time).
(Wait seven seconds.)

7. Please begin. Follow the direction.
(Allow students to begin.)

8. Thank you.

INTERVENTION 31: CHECK-IN CHART WITH TALK LATER CARDS

Misbehavior: Avoiding Social Interactions

Essential Components of Behavior Intervention Addressed

- Attention and relationship
- Signal, warn, restate
- Be flexible
- Provide choices

Need:

- 3 × 3 Sticky Notes
- Chart Paper or Folder
- *Talk Later* Cards

Know:

Teachers are often the first line of support for students and the people they confide in if a situation in the school needs adult intervention. Because it can be difficult for teachers to know how students are feeling and thinking, this intervention helps those who want to talk about their feelings. If, for example, a student needs five minutes to themselves at the beginning of class, it is good to know rather than precipitate a confrontation.

Explain to students that if they ever tell you anything about harming themselves or others, you are obligated to seek further help for them. Discuss this strategy with your campus counselor/social worker so that you are familiar with any warning signs for students experiencing crises and so you know all guidelines your district has for confidentiality and getting help for at-risk students.

Do:

1. Create an open folder or a chart (like figure 7.36) divided into sections that describe feelings.
2. Place it behind or near your desk so that it is accessible to students. Next to the chart, place a pen and a stack of extra sticky notes.
3. When students enter the classroom and are settling down, pass out one sticky note to each student and ask them to write their names on the back of the sticky note. They should place their sticky note so that their name does not show in the section of the chart that matches their feelings.
4. Explain to students that you want to know if they are in a bad mood, need someone to talk to, are upset about something, or have other concerns.
5. Take a quick look at the sticky notes and follow up with any student who wants a check-in with an adult. If there isn't time to talk at that moment, set a time for a brief talk at the end of class, lunch time, or the end of the day.
6. Use the *Talk Later* Cards to remind the student.
7. Refer the student to the counselor or social worker if they seem to be in distress or need intensive support.

Figure 7.36 Check-In Chart With Talk Later Cards

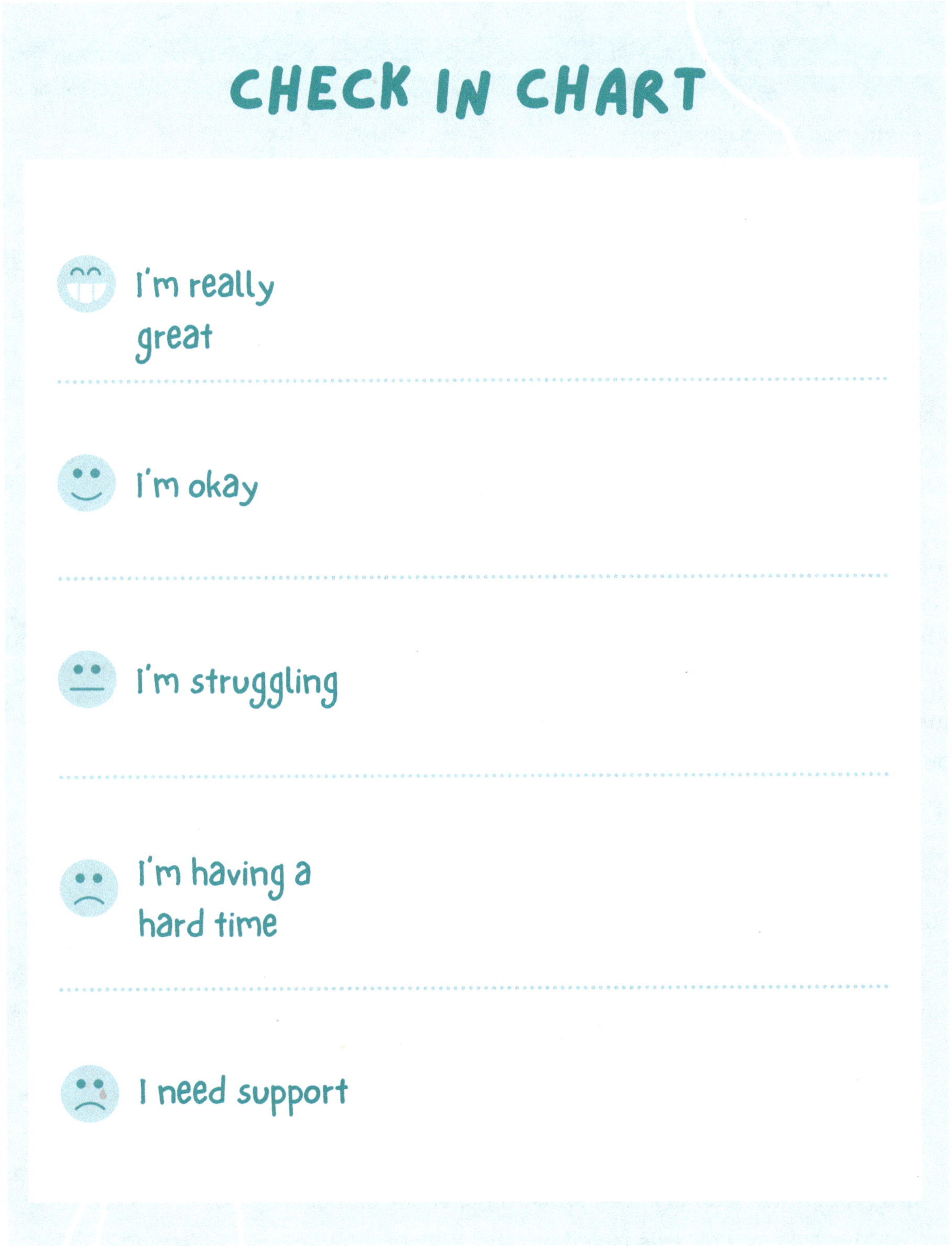

CHECK IN CHART

I'm really great

I'm okay

I'm struggling

I'm having a hard time

I need support

Avoiding Social Interactions

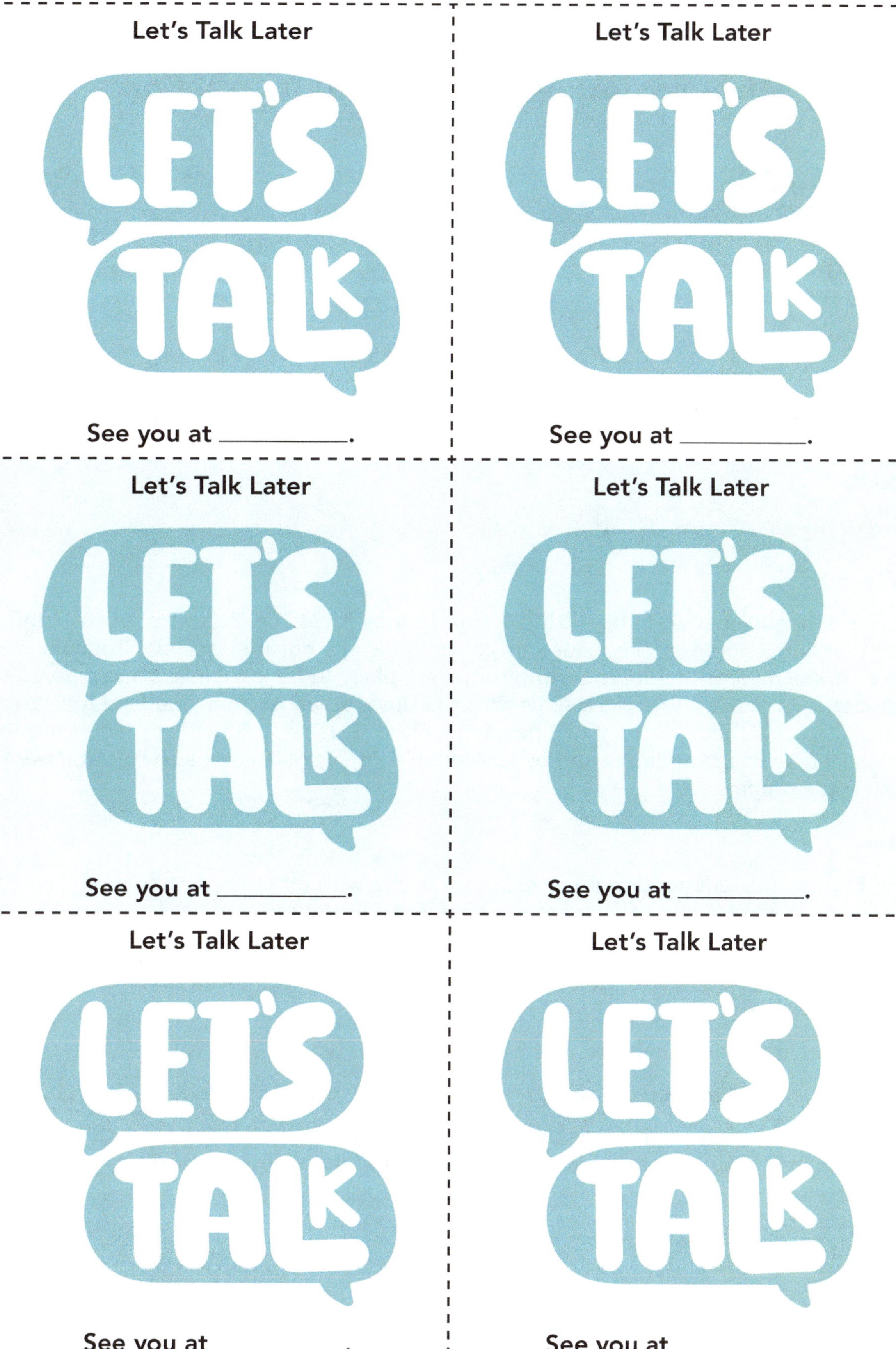

Image source: Istock.com/Igor Levin

Avoiding Social Interactions

INTERVENTION 32: PARTNER DO'S

Misbehavior: Avoiding Social Interactions

Essential Components of Behavior Intervention Addressed

- Signal, warn, restate
- Teach/reteach
- Be flexible
- Provide choices

Need:

- *Partner Do's* Prompt Card

Know:

When students have trouble fitting into a group, it can be awkward, even painful, for everyone. However, the issues in group work are not just social. Students who have problems working in and with groups are likely to have their academic progress impacted as well. Partner work skills are sometimes different from small or large group skills because there are only two people involved. It is very difficult to hide from the other person or remain quiet and be ignored. It's important to break the ice and establish some rapport.

Do:

1. Explain to students that a key skill in working with others is getting ready for partner work.
2. Pass out the *Partner Do's* Prompt Card (figure 7.37) and review the five behaviors described on the card. Stress how important they are for social acceptance and friendships.
3. Model and rehearse the behaviors in the steps if necessary.
4. Tell students to keep the card near them as they work so they can refer to it.
5. At the end of the activity, ask each student to review their behavior with their partner and briefly say what they might want to do differently next time.

Figure 7.37 Partner Do's Prompt Card

Front	Back
 Hello	Say hi or fist bump your partner
	Make small talk/do a quick check in: "Hey! How's it going?" "What's up?"
	Share something: What is happening at home How you are feeling If you can't think of anything else . . . the weather, lunch
	Acknowledge your partner's response: "That's great!" "Sorry to hear that." "That's interesting."
	Finished? Pay the person a compliment and have a seat. Start your partner work.

Image sources: Istock.com/ Vera Kostyleva, istock.com/snipergraphic, Istock.com/ Catur Nurhadi, Istock.com/najimu and wlstock.com/Tanya St

INTERVENTION 33: EVERYONE IS IN

Misbehavior: Avoiding Social Interactions

Essential Components of Behavior Intervention Addressed

- Be flexible
- Change the environment
- Use positive reinforcement
- Provide choices

Need:

- *Everyone Is In* Role Sheet

Know:

Avoiding Social Interactions

Assigning students to groups is an instructional decision that should be made by the teacher, not the student. While there may be a very limited number of situations in which students can select someone to work with, in most cases, the teacher should decide who works with whom and what each person's role is. It is also important to consider how long you want groups to work together. In some cases, the same groups can work together for a lesson, and other times they can work together for a week or more. Keep in mind that students who avoid socialization and isolate themselves need practice at social skills that they may find difficult.

Do:

1. Use the *Everyone Is In* Role Sheet (figure 7.38) to assign each group member a role so that all students are included in the group work.
2. Consider these and other types of student characteristics when assigning students to work together: Outgoing/Shy, Talker/Quiet, Artistic/Analytical, Good Writer/Likes to Draw/Enjoys Math, Dominates Conversation/Doesn't Like to Talk, Perfectionistic/Sloppy, and Nervous/Confident.
3. Model and rehearse what the role looks like, sounds like.
4. Encourage, greeter, reviewer, introducer, friend to new people, explorer, and reporter to the class are roles that are helpful for and should be practiced by students who are withdrawn or isolated.
5. Look for students who are having difficulty with socializing. Make sure they are not isolated. Switch out groups so all students get to know each other.

Figure 7.38 Everyone Is In Role Sheet

Encourager*	Recorder	Timekeeper	Materials Manager
Note Taker	Greeter*	Introducer*	Reporter to the Class*
Referee	Reviewer*	Friend to New People*	Direction Explainer
Wild Card	Checker	Explorer*	Runner

*Roles that encourage socialization

INTERVENTION 34: TIME TICKETS

Misbehavior: Avoiding Social Interactions

Essential Components of Behavior Intervention Addressed

- Be flexible
- Use positive reinforcement
- Provide choices

Need:

- *Time Tickets*

Know:

For some students, just talking to another person is difficult. As you teach students and encourage them to converse and participate with others, you should use positive reinforcement to build and maintain their new social skills. Giving students time to do something they choose is a very powerful reinforcer and *Time Tickets* make this reinforcement easy.

Do:

1. Explain to students that they will earn tickets for socialization and participation with others.
2. Ask students to choose an activity they prefer or a job they like to do. Some options, include:
    - Work with a buddy
    - Time on your iPad or laptop
    - Help another student
    - Compliment someone
    - Call a loved one and brag
    - Read aloud to younger students
    - Sit at teacher's desk
    - Skip a math problem
    - Brag to the principal
3. Give tickets (figure 7.39) to students who model positive socialization skills.
4. Provide students opportunities to trade in their tickets after a lesson or an activity to do something they like or socialize with other students.
5. The *Time Tickets* include activities that most students enjoy, but add other activities you know that your students prefer.

Figure 7.39 Time Tickets

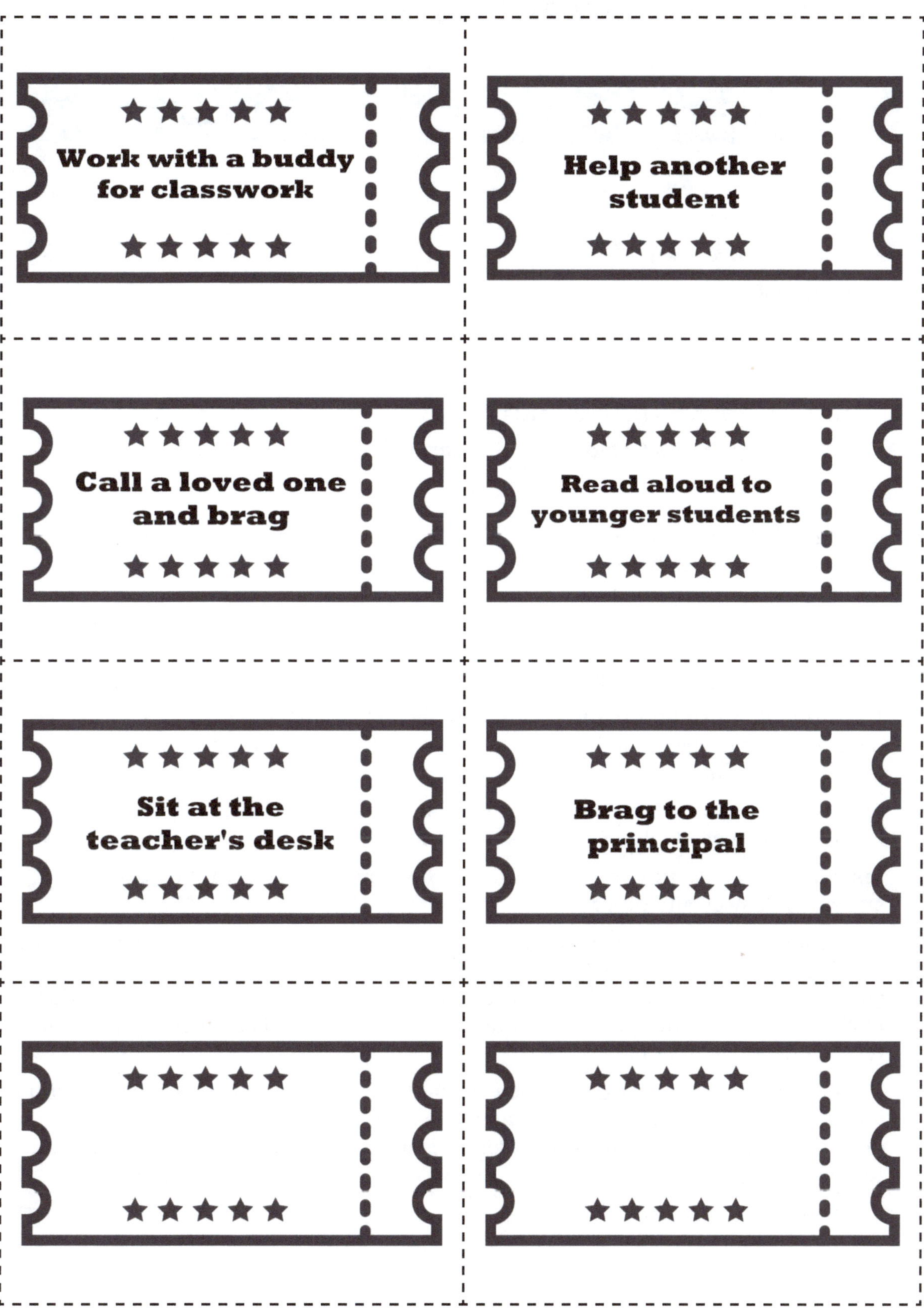

Image source: Istock.com/LysenkoAlexander

Avoiding Social Interactions

INTERVENTION 35: INSIDE/OUTSIDE CIRCLES

Misbehavior: Avoiding Social Interactions

Essential Components of Behavior Intervention Addressed

- Teach/reteach
- Be flexible
- Change the environment
- Provide choices

Avoiding Social Interactions

Need:

- *Inside/Outside Circles Review* Cards
- *Inside/Outside Circles Get to Know You* Cards

Know:

Inside/Outside Circles can be used two ways: to review learning and to encourage students to get to know each other.

Do:

1. To review instructional content, ask each student to write a review question for the current lesson, unit, or reading on the *Review* Cards (figure 7.40).
2. Tell students to stand up and create two big circles (moving furniture first if you have to) so that one circle is inside another. Half your students should be in one inside circle; half should be in the outside circle.
3. Ask the students to face each other, so that students in the inside circle are facing out and students in the outside circle are facing in.
4. Instruct the inside students to ask their question and listen to the outside student's answer and discuss.
5. After each question and discussion, tell the students in the outside circle to rotate clockwise (or counterclockwise, one step, two steps, etc.), so they are across from someone new. Alternate with who asks their questions first, the students in the inside circle or the students in the outside. Continue in this fashion until all the review questions have been asked.
6. To encourage students to get to know each other, ask students to write a question for their classmates on the *Get to Know You* Cards. Share some guidelines, such as don't ask questions that are too personal, embarrassing, or inappropriate. Prompt them to ask questions like, "What's your favorite song?" or "Do you have a pet?"
7. Follow steps two to five.

Figure 7.40 Inside/Outside Circles Cards

REVIEW CARDS	
My review question:	My review question:
My review question:	My review question:
My review question:	My review question:

Avoiding Social Interactions

Avoiding Social Interactions

GET TO KNOW YOU CARDS	
What pets do you have? What are they? How did you get them? What are their names? What tricks can they do?	How many brothers and sisters do you have? What are their names? What do you like to do with them?
What is your favorite movie? Why? What are your favorite movie stars? Why? What would you do with them if you could spend a day with them?	What's your favorite sports team? Why? Who are your favorite players? Why?
What's your favorite restaurant? What do you like to eat there? When do you go?	Who do you look up to in your family? Who do you admire most? Why?
If you could meet anyone famous, who would it be? What would you do with them?	What is your favorite place to be? Why? What do you like to do there?

INTERVENTION 36: MY WORRY PLAN

Misbehavior: Failing to Cope With Typical Classroom Expectations Because of Worries and Perfectionism

Essential Components of Behavior Intervention Addressed

- Attention and relationship
- Teach/reteach
- Be flexible
- Change the environment
- Provide choices

Need:

- *My Worry Plan* Form

Know:

My Worry Plan is a practical and easy-to-implement intervention that supports students who have a history of worrying too much to the extent that it causes them physical health problems, damages their social relationships, and/or interferes with their learning. They may fear failing and procrastinate or their perfectionism keeps them from starting and working on assignments.

Do:

1. Discuss the suggestions on the *My Worry Plan* forms (figure 7.41) with the student when they tell you (or you can tell) that they are agitated, withdrawn, nervous, or anxious.
2. Review the actions they can take when they start to worry too much and can't stop themselves.
3. Set up a visit to the counselor, social worker, or other resource, who can discuss and model some of the actions the student can take, if warranted.
4. After students use the form, take some time to discuss it with them, asking them how they did, what worked and what didn't work, and how they can address their worries next time.
5. Follow up by checking with them to see if there are other ways you can remind them or support them as they use the strategies in *My Worry Plan*.

Figure 7.41 My Worry Plan for Primary and Intermediate Grade Students

PLAN FOR PRIMARY GRADE STUDENTS

My Worry Plan 1

Name ______________________ **Date** ______________

How worried are you? Circle the face that matches how you feel.

happy meh sad anxious scared

Draw what you are worried about.

How can you make this worry smaller on your own? Check as many ideas as you want. You can also add your own ideas.

- ☐ I can practice deep breathing exercise.
- ☐ I can imagine myself outside in the park, on a trail, on the beach, or in the mountains.
- ☐ I can imagine myself doing things with people I love.
- ☐ I can draw pictures of things I'm glad I have.
- ☐ I can call or play with friends or family.
- ☐ I can ______________________

____

When can we talk about how you're doing? Let's choose a date: ______________

Source: Used with permission of Teacher Created Materials, Inc, from Help Anxious Kids in a Stressful World : 25 Classroom Strategies, David Campos and Kathleen McConnell Fad, 1st edition, 2023; permission conveyed through Copyright Clearance Center, Inc.

PLAN FOR INTERMEDIATE GRADE STUDENTS

My Worry Plan 2

Name ______________________________ **Date** ________________

How worried are you? Circle the number that matches how you feel.

1	2	3	4	5
not at all worried	not worried	not sure	a little worried	very worried

Write about or draw what is worrying you.

How can you make this worry smaller on your own? Check as many ideas as you want. You can also add your own ideas.

- ☐ I can practice deep breathing exercise.
- ☐ I can visualize myself in nature.
- ☐ I can visualize myself doing things with people I love.
- ☐ I can draw and write in my gratitude journal.
- ☐ I can do something nice for myself.
- ☐ I can call or hang out with friends or loved ones.
- ☐ I can draw a picture of my worries and label the emotions I have.
- ☐ I can ______________________________
____

Ask your trusted adult to check on your progress. Choose a specific date: ________________

INTERVENTION 37: WORRY BREAKS

Misbehavior: Failing to Cope With Typical Classroom Expectations Because of Worries and Perfectionism

Essential Components of Behavior Intervention Addressed

- Signal, warn, restate
- Be flexible
- Change the environment
- Provide choices

Need:

- *Worry Breaks* Menu and Signal Cards
- Timer

Know:

When a student is worrying too much, getting nervous, or feeling afraid, use the *Worry Breaks* signal cards to signal a break. At that moment, the student can visit an area of the room—a center or table—to use age-appropriate sensory items and fidget toys (see Intervention 10) to distract them from their worries and thoughts. Before using this intervention, make sure that students understand that the purpose is to interrupt their stream of worry—to stop worrying and think of something else. This intervention shows them one way to cope with their worries and perfectionism. Often, students are not able to stop worrying on their own, so using a fidget toy or sensory item can take their mind off their worry.

Do:

1. Explain to the student who worries too much that an area is available for them when they feel overwhelmed with worry.
2. Review the items on the menu (figure 7.42) as options to distract the student.
3. Point to the *You Need a Break* card or put the card on the student's desk to show that they can visit the center.
4. Provide *I Need a Break* cards for the student to show you when they need to use the center.
5. Set a timer for five to seven minutes to track the time when the student is at the center.
6. Allow the student to visit the center.
7. Create new guidelines and conference with the student if this intervention is being used too frequently.

Figure 7.42 Worry Breaks Menu and Signal Cards

WORRY BREAKS MENU

- ☐ Use the hearing protection earmuffs to cancel out classroom noise.
- ☐ Use the headphones to listen to soft music or white noise.
- ☐ Watch a calming video of the wind in the trees, the ocean, or clouds.
- ☐ Watch livecams of ocean animals.
- ☐ Sit and use some quiet fidget toys.
- ☐ Smell the scented markers.
- ☐ Play with the slime.
- ☐ Play with the calming bottle.
- ☐ Rub the suede, the faux fur, or sequin fabric.
- ☐ Look at photos of birds, flowers, rocks, baby animals, and others.
- ☐ Look at photos of mountains, beaches, jungles, and forests.
- ☐ ______________________
- ☐ ______________________

You Need a Break

Pick Something From the Menu

I Need a Break

Can I Pick Something From the Menu?

You Need a Break

Pick Something From the Menu

I Need a Break

Can I Pick Something From the Menu?

Image source: Istock.com/flavijus

INTERVENTION 38: VISUALIZE IT

Misbehavior: Failing to Cope With Typical Classroom Expectations Because of Worries and Perfectionism

Essential Components of Behavior Intervention Addressed

- Signal, warn, restate
- Teach/reteach
- Change the environment
- Provide choices

Need:

- Calming Images and Videos

Know:

One way to distract children's negative thinking (like an unhealthy fear of failure) is to have a picture in our mind that we can relate to and visualize. This strategy can help children, too. When students are worrying too much, some images can allow them to form a mental picture of themselves and let go of their worries. Like Intervention 37, this strategy helps them learn how to cope with their worrying.

Do:

1. Select some images for display that can help students with visualization. The images should be relatable and not too abstract. Here are some options that represents the elimination or releasing of worries:
   - A fish swimming in a whirlpool of bubbles and swimming away from them leaving them behind
   - Holding on to a bunch of balloons and letting them fly away into the sky
   - A train chugging up a steep mountain, making its way to the top, and slowly disappearing down the tracks
   - A sailboat in rough seas slowly gliding away into the tranquil horizon while
   - Threatening storm clouds being slowly carried away by the wind
   - Candles in paper lanterns floating up into the sky until they disappear
2. Select the images with the students that can help them imagine releasing their worries.
3. Explain that the images can help them visualize the release of their worries so that they can think of something else.
4. Use a script like this to help them with the visualization:

   "Imagine you are a fish and you are swimming along, but in front of you are a bunch of bubbles. They are always there, getting in your way. Instead of letting them bother you, swim through and away from them. Your worries are gone and you can think of something else and have the focus and energy to do something else."

5. Explore YouTube® using "calming videos for children" in the search bar for other ideas and sources to show the students.

INTERVENTION 39: REJECT AND REPLACE

Misbehavior: Failing to Cope With Typical Classroom Expectations Because of Worries and Perfectionism

Essential Components of Behavior Intervention Addressed

- Signal, warn, restate
- Teach/reteach
- Be flexible

Need:

- *Reject and Replace* Cards

Know:

It can be difficult to convince students who worry too much that their worries are unfounded, that worrying doesn't help or solve any problems, or that it is a waste of time. Despite the difficulty, it is important to talk to students about these issues and share tools to reduce worrying so that they can relax, relate to their peers more easily, and focus on academics and instruction. *Reject and Replace* is a tool that can help students decide if they can do anything about their worries or if their perfectionism is out of their control. If a student can't do anything about a worry, then they may be able to see the logic in rejecting that worry and replacing it with a positive thought.

Do:

1. Talk about which of their worries the student can do something about. For example, worrying about their mom getting sick is not something they can control. But they can control other worries, such as worrying about passing a test (they can study for it). Other examples include the following:
   - They can't control a storm, but they can prepare for it by wearing the right clothing and/or taking shelter.
   - They can't control getting sick, but they can eat healthy and exercise regularly.
   - They can't control losing a friend, but they can show positive social skills to keep their friendship.
   - They can't control having to move schools, but they can think about the new friends they will make.
   - They can't control when they will see a loved one again, but they can write letters, draw pictures, or make small gifts for them, so they have something to give them when they see them again.

2. Discuss other kinds of thoughts they can use to replace the worries that they can't control. For example, to try and stop their worrying they can think about some of these ideas: something they are grateful for or appreciate, what they would do if they could spend the day with a loved one, planning a birthday party for a pet, how they might improve the classroom, or giving an award to someone special.
3. Copy the *Reject and Replace* Cards (figure 7.43) and give each student a few or place them where students can easily find them.
4. Ask students to identify what they are worried about. Discuss each worry, decide if they can do anything about it, and if not, replace it with a positive thought.

Figure 7.43 Reject and Replace Cards

MY WORRIES	DO I HAVE CONTROL OVER MY WORRIES?	WHAT CAN I THINK ABOUT INSTEAD?
I worry about: ____________________ ____________________	Yes No	☐ Something good that happened today ☐ A friend ☐ My dog/cat/pet ☐ Someone who is nice to me ☐ A great lunch today ☐ Fun at recess ☐ Helping the teacher ☐ Doing a good job on my school work ☐ The fun I had ____________ ☐ Other ____________ ☐ Other ____________
I worry about: ____________________ ____________________	Yes No	☐ Something good that happened today ☐ A friend ☐ My dog/cat/pet ☐ Someone who is nice to me ☐ A great lunch today ☐ Fun at recess ☐ Helping the teacher ☐ Doing a good job on my school work ☐ The fun I had ____________ ☐ Other ____________ ☐ Other ____________

INTERVENTION 40: PERSONAL PLAN B

Misbehavior: Failing to Cope With Typical Classroom Expectations Because of Worries and Perfectionism

Essential Components of Behavior Intervention Addressed

- Attention and relationship
- Teach/reteach
- Be flexible
- Provide choices

Need:

- *Personal Plan B* Forms

Know:

When students are perfectionistic, their thinking may become rigid and they may get stuck in only one way of doing things, only one right product or response, or only one solution to a problem or question. Then, if their way of doing things does not work out, or turns out to be incorrect, or is not acceptable, it can trigger a strong response. Sometimes, perfectionistic students can have a "meltdown" and become angry or argumentative. They may also cry and start to call themselves or others' names. These students may also express their intention to give up, tear up or destroy their work, or throw papers or assignments in the trash. *Personal Plan B* can help prevent such unhealthy and unproductive responses.

Do:

1. Explain that no one is perfect by promoting the idea that doing one's best is a healthy, reasonable goal.
2. Copy and provide *Personal Plan B* (figure 7.44) to review with the student. Discuss the Plan B options as well as what support he student might need.
3. Give the student some choices so that they can develop their own Personal Plan B that they are comfortable with and that is reasonable for them. Help them develop their plan.
4. Discuss and practice non-catastrophic responses when things don't go as planned or perfection is not achieved.
5. Refer them to their *Personal Plan B* and support them when they feel they are not perfect or things are not going as they would like (perfect).

Figure 7.44 Personal Plan B Form

HERE ARE SOME THINGS THAT I HAVE TROUBLE WITH	HERE'S MY PERSONAL PLAN B
It bothers me when:	I can do one or more of these:
☐ I don't get 100's on an assignment.	☐ Say, "I did my best."
☐ I make a mistake.	☐ Say, "I tried hard."
☐ The teacher corrects something I did.	☐ Tell my teacher I am okay with how I did.
☐ I say something wrong in front of other people.	☐ Explain to others that I am working hard, but I made a mistake.
☐ My work isn't perfect.	☐ Tell myself that no one is perfect.
☐ I'm in a group and the other students don't accept what I say.	☐ Tell myself that I am doing really well.
☐ I get almost all the way through a problem or assignment and find out a made a mistake at the beginning.	☐ Show my parents how well I did.
☐ I don't get straight A's on my report card.	☐ Stay calm and keep trying.
☐ Other: ______________________	☐ Ask my friends for a fist bump.
☐ Other: ______________________	☐ Correct what I got wrong with a smile on my face.
	☐ Move on to the next activity.
	☐ Other: ______________________
	☐ Other: ______________________

INTERVENTION 41: JUST SAY THANKS

Misbehavior: Tantrumming to Get Their Way

Essential Components of Behavior Intervention Addressed

- Attention and relationship
- Signal, warn, restate
- Teach/reteach

Need:

- *Just Say Thanks* Cards

Know:

When students get negative or unwelcome feedback from teachers, some of them can handle it, stay calm, and move on. Unfortunately for some students, hearing a "no," a correction, or a reprimand escalates their behavior. The escalation can include arguing, refusing, yelling, crying, leaving their area, or even worse reactions as they try to get their way in the situation. One way to prevent escalations is to teach students how to respond, either positive or neutral. Teaching students to *Just Say Thanks* is a simple response that can prevent students from losing control.

Do:

1. Introduce *Just Say Thanks* (figure 7.45) to the student (or whole class) and show the cards. Explain that when you must correct them or give them bad news ("Please correct your mistakes, numbers one and three," *or* "No, you can't go to the bus early," *or* "Please sit down now; we're ready to start"), they can simply respond, "Thanks."
2. Provide examples of situations they might not want to respond to in a positive way.
3. Explain that their first step is to listen without arguing and then just say "Thanks."
4. Remind students that this response will help them maintain their positive relationships, stay calm, and move forward throughout the day with behavior problems that will likely result in serious consequences.

Figure 7.45 Just Say Thanks Cards

You may not want to hear it, but listen and just say **Thanks**	Just Say **Thanks**
You may not want to hear it, but listen and just say **Thanks**	Just Say **Thanks**
You may not want to hear it, but listen and just say **Thanks**	Just Say **Thanks**

INTERVENTION 42: IT PAYS TO SAY OK

Misbehavior: Tantrumming to Get Their Way

Essential Components of Behavior Intervention Addressed

- Attention and relationship
- Teach/reteach
- Use positive reinforcement
- Provide choices

Need:

- *It Pays to Say OK* Tickets and Reinforcement Menu

Know:

Learning to accept not getting their own way is a very difficult behavior for some students. They have mastered the art of the tantrum and have a set of responses they use at home and at school. When students are learning a new behavior that is difficult or challenging for them, it is important to use positive reinforcement to increase the likelihood of that behavior. Some positive reinforcement comes in the form of verbal praise or compliments, and some can be activity based or involve material reinforcers. Yet another option is social attention from either an adult or from other students. When teaching students to say "Okay" and accept no for an answer or to accept a consequence, it is good to link an immediate reinforcer, like a ticket or coupon, to a more valuable positive reinforcer that student may need to wait for. Both immediate and short-term positive reinforcement can be effective. This is similar to Intervention 41, but for some students, saying "okay" is going to be a lot easier than saying "thanks," so you may need to try both options. Unlike the *Just Say Thanks* Tickets, the *It Pays to Say OK* Tickets are not a prompt used before the behavior, but rather a reinforcer provided *after* the student demonstrates the behavior.

Do:

1. Reinforce the student immediately (give them each a ticket) after they say "OK" or when they accept a "no" response or when they are willing to do what is asked without losing control.
2. Fill in the *OK Menu* with items that students can buy with their tickets. The items can include a new pencil, a new eraser, special paper, and so forth. See the example.
3. Depending on the student's age, let them redeem their tickets once a day, once or twice a week, or once a week. Make sure they understand how they earned the tickets and give them some choices in the menu items.
4. The *OK Tickets* and menu are shown in figure 7.46. You can create a menu with student input to ensure that the items are motivating.

Figure 7.46 It Pays to Say OK Tickets

You said "OK" and you did OK.
Good for you

You said "OK" and you did OK.
Good for you

You said "OK" and you did OK.
Good for you

You said "OK" and you did OK.
Good for you

You said "OK" and you did OK.
Good for you

You said "OK" and you did OK.
Good for you

You said "OK" and you did OK.
Good for you

You said "OK" and you did OK.
Good for you

Image source: Istock.com/ Colorfuel Studio

OK MENU	
1.	Tickets
2.	
3.	
4.	
5.	
6.	

SAMPLE MENU	
A new pencil	5 tickets
A new eraser	5 tickets
Special drawing paper	5 tickets
Help the teacher set up the whiteboard	5 tickets
Be the pencil sharpener for a day	5 tickets
Call a loved one to celebrate how well you are doing	7 tickets
Get some time at the calming center	7 tickets
Go tell your favorite person in school how you earned the tickets	10 tickets
Be the class pet monitor for the week	10 tickets
You pick the opening game/activity at recess this week	10 tickets
Lunch in the classroom	10 tickets
Invite your parent or grandparent to lunch (The school will pay)	20 tickets
Special breakfast with the teacher	20 tickets
Your choice: ____________________	________
Your choice: ____________________	________

INTERVENTION 43: WATCH YOURSELF STAY CALM

Misbehavior: Tantrumming to Get Their Way

Essential Components of Behavior Intervention Addressed

- Teach/reteach
- Use positive reinforcement
- Provide choices

Need:

- *Watch Yourself Stay Calm* Card

Know:

When we are dealing with challenging behaviors and teaching students positive social behaviors, it is important that they are aware of how they are doing. One way to help students track their progress is to teach them to self-monitor. All students can learn to check their own behavior and almost all can track it themselves, so they see their progress and recognize it. To help students self-monitor as they learn to accept "no" and react calmly when they don't get their own way, this intervention includes two trackers, one for younger students or short-term monitoring and one that allows for a little longer tracking.

Do:

1. Provide a tracker (such as figure 7.47) to a student who is improving at staying calm. The forms may not appeal to older students. In such cases, search the Internet for images of interests they may have, like superheroes, pop stars, or famous athletes. Print a selected image and cut it up like a puzzle.
2. Each time the student accepts no, stays calm, says okay or something like it, and does not tantrum to get their own way, tell them to connect a line on the tracker. Older students can get a puzzle piece to put together to determine what their celebrity is doing.
3. When they reach the end, allow them to select from a menu of privileges (see Intervention 42 *It Pays to Say OK* for an example).

Figure 7.47 Watch Yourself Stay Calm Cards

Name: Date:

Behavior Title:

Tantrumming to Get Their Way

INTERVENTION 44: SAY NO SILENTLY

Misbehavior: Tantrumming to Get Their Way

Essential Components of Behavior Intervention Addressed

- Attention and relationship
- Signal, warn, restate
- Teach/reteach
- Be flexible
- Change the environment

Need:

- Poster With Silent Signs

Know:

When a student uses a tantrum to get their way, teacher attention and intervention can sometimes make the situation worse instead of better. Saying "no" to the student, reprimanding, or reminding them of what they *should* be doing could escalate students who seek attention, regardless of the kind or quality of the attention. To head the escalation off, give less attention to the student, and still communicate, using silent signs can be invaluable. Teachers can use this intervention with one student or the whole class, and the silent signs can be used in many situations, not just when a student is having problems with self-control.

Do:

1. Make a large poster of the signs in the reproducible (figure 7.48) and/or project them on the whiteboard:
   - The American Sign Language (ASL) sign for "Stop."
   - The ASL sign for "No."
   - The "shhh" sign with finger to your lips.
   - Hold up a red stop sign or place a small version on the student's desk.
   - Hold up your open hand, with your palm facing the student, meaning "calm down" or "take it easy."
2. Explain to students when and how you will use the signs before using them.
3. Leave the sign posted for reference.
4. Give them examples of when you will use the signs. Tell them that when you use them, you are not ignoring them, but rather communicating in a way that should help them regain control without bothering other students or disrupting instruction.

Figure 7.48 Say No Silently Sign

This means STOP.	 stop
This means NO.	 no
This means QUIET.	 QUIET PLEASE
This means STOP.	 STOP
This means CALM DOWN or TAKE IT EASY.	

Image sources: Istock.com/SurfUpVector and Istock.com/:Christian Horz

INTERVENTION 45: AFTER AND BEFORE

Misbehavior: Tantrumming to Get Their Way

Essential Components of Behavior Intervention Addressed

- Attention and relationship
- Teach/reteach
- Provide choices

Need:

- *After and Before* Form

Know:

Teachers should never try to teach behavior in the middle of a crisis or when a student is emotionally distraught or out of control. Learning will not happen in those situations. However, after a student de-escalates, it is important to follow up with the student and process what happened. This follow-up is to help the student be honest about what they did, why they did it, and what they can do differently next time. It always helps to have some questions ready to guide this type of difficult discussion. Use an *After and Before* Form to guide the student as they process after an escalation. Two versions of the *After and Before* form are provided, one for younger students and nonreaders and one for older students.

If the student has been aggressive or lost control, an administrator, guidance counselor, behavior specialist, or social worker may also talk the student through the incident and follow up.

Do:

1. Wait until the student has calmed down.
2. Find a five-to-ten-minute block of time to have one-on-one time with the student.
3. Use the appropriate form (figure 7.49) with the student to describe what they did and what precipitated their behavior. Identify what they wanted and whether they got it. (As an alternative, use the questions on the form for a discussion, but ask the student to reflect on what happened by drawing or writing about the incident. They could write it in a journal so that the two of you can later look at progress or to help you determine whether additional support is warranted).
4. Discuss what they can do differently next time and what kind of help they need to succeed.
5. If the student can tell what new behavior they are going to try, identify it and add it to their daily goals or create a reminder card.
6. Remind the student during the week what they need to work on and follow up to celebrate success or provide additional support.

Figure 7.49 After and Before Forms for Younger Students/Nonreaders and Older Students

FOR YOUNGER STUDENTS AND NONREADERS

Name ______________________________ **Date** ______________

After and Before

1. What did you do?

   Draw or place a picture of your behavior.

2. Why did you do this?

   Draw or place a picture of what happened or how you were feeling.

3. What did you want to happen?

   Draw or place a picture of what you wanted.

4. What will you do differently next time?

   Draw yourself doing something different.

5. Who can help you?

   Draw a picture of someone you can ask for help.

6. Can you do it?  

Sign your name here. ______________________________

The adult will sign here. ______________________________

Source: After and Before (Adapted) From *Positive Alternatives to Restrain and Seclusion for Aggressive Kids* (p. 181, 182), by Kathleen McConnell, Katherine O. Synatschk, 2012, Austin, TX: PRO-ED. Copyright 2012 by PRO-ED, Inc. Adapted with permission.

FOR OLDER STUDENTS

After and Before

1. What did you do? Describe your behavior.

___

___

2. What happened right before you behaved this way?

___

___

3. What did you want? (e.g., Attention/control/get out of class/avoid the assignment/get back at the adult/get revenge for something/to get sent home/don't know)

___

4. Did you get what you wanted? YES NO

5. What can you do differently next time this situation occurs?

___

___

6. What help will you need?

___

___

7. Who would you like to help you?

___

8. How can you ask for this help?

___

9. Do you think you can be successful at this new behavior? YES NO

Student Signature: ___

Adult Signature: ___

Source: After and Before (Adapted) From *Positive Alternatives to Restrain and Seclusion for Aggressive Kids* (p. 181, 182), by Kathleen McConnell, Katherine O. Synatschk, 2012, Austin, TX: PRO-ED.

INTERVENTION 46: A PLAN TO GET ALONG

Misbehavior: Violating Classroom Norms to the Point of Negatively Impacting Others

Essential Components of Behavior Intervention Addressed

- Attention and relationship
- Teach/reteach
- Provide choices

Need:

- *A Plan to Get Along* Form

Know:

It is always easier to prevent student misbehavior than to deal with it after it begins. This is especially true when students refuse to follow directions and do so defiantly. No one wants to deal with such a situation. Most students will not need specific interventions related to this behavior, but for those who do, having a plan is important.

Do:

1. Have a copy of the *A Plan to Get Along* form (figure 7.50).
2. Help the student identify the triggers, or antecedents to their behavior: What sets them off? What upsets them? What is it that makes them want to refuse to do what adults ask them to do? Write and discuss the information calmly.
3. Talk about when these situations arise and how they usually react.
4. Help the student make a practical plan for dealing with their own defiance. What can they do? How should they handle it? If they know they will get in trouble, why do they defy authority anyway? Focus on realistic, practical options like walking away, staying quiet, and other calm reactions.
5. Read the form aloud to the student whenever practical. It is not just about completing the form; the conversation is important.
6. Make sure the student understands their options and then remind them each morning or several times a day of the plan. This is a good discussion to have during their morning or class check-in time.
7. Make sure you recognize their hard work and reinforce them for their progress when the student starts to improve and follow their plan.
8. If a counselor or social worker has a special relationship with the student, involve them as well.

Figure 7.50 A Plan to Get Along Form

USE THIS FORM WHEN THE STUDENT IS CALM

MAKE A PLAN FOR DEALING WITH SITUATIONS WHEN THE STUDENT DOES NOT WANT TO DO WHAT AN ADULT TELLS THEM TO DO

Teacher: Let's talk about these questions together. Either you can write your responses, or I can write them." Then we'll make a plan.

1. What makes you so upset that you don't want to follow directions? Is it that . . . You can't do the work? . . . You don't like being told what to do? . . . You think you know everything already and what the teacher asks you to do is stupid? Other reasons?

____

____

____

____

2. Let's make a plan so that you start to go along with what adults tell you to do. You will learn more, and you will not get in trouble and face serious consequences. I will help you with this plan.

Would you like to . . .

☐ Ask for a break?

☐ Talk to an adult alone? If so, who?

☐ Do a two-minute head down? Put your head down and take two minutes?

☐ Do some deep breathing?

☐ Sit in a quiet area to do your work?

☐ Other? ______________________

☐ Other? ______________________

Pick at least one choice in Number two. You can signal me with a "break" sign, tell me privately, or sit at your desk and put your head down or breathe deeply. Then you will need to do what an adult asks you to do.

INTERVENTION 47: DE-STRESS

Misbehavior: Violating Classroom Norms to the Point of Negatively Impacting Others

Essential Components of Behavior Intervention Addressed

- Attention and relationship
- Signal, warn, restate
- Teach/reteach
- Be flexible
- Change the environment
- Use positive reinforcement
- Provide choices

Need:

- *Signals of Stress* List
- *De-Stress Movements*
- *My Personal De-Stress Plan*

Know:

Student agitation is often physical as well as emotional and behavioral. Students may not always recognize that they are both emotionally and physically stressed, so they may need to be taught to recognize the physical signals of stress. Getting physically calm may, in turn, reduce the likelihood that the student will escalate to serious behaviors. This intervention includes three reproducibles, which can be used as a set to help students learn their own personal signals of stress, what to do to de-stress, and then make a personal plan. If stress is the cause of their escalating noncompliance, de-stressing should help them. Additional ideas are provided in the Teach Calming Techniques section of chapter 4.

Do:

1. Teach students how to recognize when they are physically stressed using the *Signals of Stress* List (figure 7.51).
2. Talk about which specific physical signs they recognize. Not everyone feels stress the same way.
3. Review the *Signals of Stress* with the student and ask them to identify as many of the signals that impact them as they can.
4. Review the *De-Stress Movements* List and help them choose some options they are comfortable using, first with supervision and then on their own.
5. Help the student design their own personal de-stress plan and then coach them regularly to use it on the *My Personal De-Stress Plan*.

Figure 7.51 Signals of Stress, De-Stress Movements, and My Personal De-Stress Plan

SIGNALS OF STRESS

WHEN I AM STRESSED, I FEEL (CIRCLE THE SIGNAL)		
Fidgety	Sweaty	Shaky
Like I Can't Breathe	Hot	Cold
Like I Breathe Too Fast	Red in the Face	Jumpy
Tight in the Chest	Like I Have a Headache	Wobbly
Like My Heart is Racing	Like I Can't Move	Like Crying
Like I Will Throw Up	Like My Mouth Is Dry	Wound Up

DE-STRESS MOVEMENTS

TRY THESE TO DE-STRESS:	
	☐ **Loosen Your Neck:** Stand with feet apart and gently move your head up and down, then side to side. Then bend your ear toward your shoulder. Breathe a full breath with each movement.
	☐ **Shrug Your Shoulders:** Stand with feet apart and move your shoulders up and down, forward and back, and then in circles. Breathe a full breath with each movement.
	☐ **Take a Walk:** With teacher permission, walk slowly up and down an empty hallway or along the wall of the gym. Take deep breaths as you walk. See if you can match your steps to your breathing.
	☐ **Deep Breathing:** There are lots of ways to do deep breathing. Here's a simple one that you don't need any practice to do: Breathe in slowly while counting to four in your head. Hold your breath for a count of four. Then let your breath out slowly for another count of four.

Other Ideas:

☐ Listen to calm music.

☐ Hold a fidget toy.

☐ Stretch.

☐ Put my head on my desk and close my eyes.

☐ ______________________________

Image source: Istock.com/lioputra; Istock.com/nicoletaionescu

MY PERSONAL DE-STRESS PLAN

MY PERSONAL DE-STRESS PLAN

When I feel this type of stress:

I will do this to de-stress:

If I need help I will:

INTERVENTION 48: SHOW THEM CALM

Misbehavior: Violating Classroom Norms to the Point of Negatively Impacting Others

Essential Components of Behavior Intervention Addressed

- Attention and relationship
- Signal, warn, restate
- Be flexible
- Change the environment
- Provide choices

Need:

- *Show Them Calm* Card

Know:

When a student has escalated to the point of active defiance and refusal of directions, it is difficult for those around them to stay calm. Sometimes, adults automatically react with their own escalation—a loud voice, threats, or ultimatums. Usually, those reactions make things worse instead of better. When others escalate, the student is less likely to begin to calm down and may instead escalate further, so the best thing for adults to do is *Show Them Calm*. It may take practice to model calmness in the face of anger, direct defiance, and refusals to follow directions (especially in the classroom), but that is exactly what teachers should practice and try to do. This Intervention provides a teacher cue card with a list of steps to practice and demonstrate.

Do:

1. Keep the cue card (figure 7.52) nearby and refer to it quickly before dealing with a student who has escalated to verbal aggression.
2. Follow the steps on the card when the student's behavior has escalated:
   - Speak in a soft voice.
   - Give the student some space.
   - Give the student some time (five to seven minutes, depending on student age).
   - Say, "We can talk later."
3. Follow up to discuss the issues afterwards.

Figure 7.52 Show Them Calm Card

Image source: Istock.com/ lemono; adapted from Istock.com/irem soyler

INTERVENTION 49: DO THESE INSTEAD

Misbehavior: Violating Classroom Norms to the Point of Negatively Impacting Others

Essential Components of Behavior Intervention Addressed

- Attention and relationship
- Signal, warn, restate
- Teach/reteach
- Be flexible
- Use positive reinforcement
- Provide choices

Need:

- *Do These Instead* Form
- *You Did It!* Tickcts

Know:

It is difficult to get students to totally stop a behavior that has a specific intention. They will often replace that behavior with another one that has the same purpose. For example, when students are stressed and don't know how to deal with their stress, they may yell and curse. If they finally stop cursing and yelling, they may start crying and hiding instead. It is critical that teachers teach replacement behaviors so that if one behavior decreases or gets less frequent, the behavior that replaces it is positive and acceptable, not another disruptive, antisocial behavior.

Do:

1. Teach the student prosocial behaviors like:
   - Following adults' directions
   - Expressing feelings with words
   - Accepting correction or feedback
2. Review the reproducible (figure 7.53) with the student. Adapt it to align with other selected prosocial behaviors.
3. Use a *Looks Like/Sounds Like* chart (See Intervention 16) with the student and decide what these three replacement behaviors look and sound like. If you have other replacement behaviors that match the student's needs better, use those instead.
4. Explain that you will be asking them to check themselves and record how they are doing each day for class period (for younger students, do this more frequently).

5. Give a copy of the reproducible (figure 7.53) to the student. Set an individual goal with the student, then check in with them at the end of each day or class period. If the student is doing well and making progress, use positive reinforcement choices on the *You Did It!* tickets (figure 7.54) to increase and sustain the new behaviors.

Figure 7.53 Do These Instead Form

DO THESE INSTEAD TRACKING FORM		
INSTEAD OF YELLING, CURSING, OR THREATENING, DO THESE INSTEAD AND TRACK YOURSELF		
TODAY'S DATE ____________	HOW DID YOU DO?	
	MORNING	AFTERNOON
Follow Adults' Directions	Meh Ok Great	Meh Ok Great
Express Your Feelings with Words	Meh Ok Great	Meh Ok Great
Accept Correction and Feedback	Meh Ok Great	Meh Ok Great

Figure 7.54 You Did It! Tickets

Sit in Your Favorite Spot for 10 Minutes

Listen to Music on Headphones for 10 Minutes

Lunch With Your Buddy

Call Someone and Brag About Yourself

Pick a Prize From Our Prize Box

Work With a Buddy on an Assignment Today

Give the Directions to Class Before We Go to Recess

Personal Time to Read, Draw, or Do a Puzzle

Image source: Istock.com/Fafarumba

INTERVENTION 50: FORGIVE AND MOVE ON

Misbehavior: Violating Classroom Norms to the Point of Negatively Impacting Others

Essential Components of Behavior Intervention Addressed

- Attention and relationship
- Be flexible

Need:

- *Forgive and Move On* Teacher Reminder Cards

Know:

Dealing with the most difficult behaviors in a busy classroom can be frustrating and tiring. It is natural to get angry, frustrated, nervous, hurt, and stressed by the situations you face in the classroom every day. However, medical and psychological research finds that holding on to negative feelings can be damaging to your physical health and mental wellness. Health professionals suggest letting go of grudges and forgiving those who hurt or injure us psychologically. It is important to forgive and move on, not just because of the health benefits, but also because the students you have will likely be there for the whole school year and it is best to start each day with a clean slate—fresh and ready to make a difference. Staying upset with a student will only consume the very energy you need to teach.

Do:

1. Copy the cards (figure 7.55, or make your own) to help you start each new day with a clean slate for everyone, including yourself.
2. Keep the *Forgive and Move On* Cards visible.
3. Read them regularly, as part of your daily schedule.

Figure 7.55 Forgive and Move On Cards

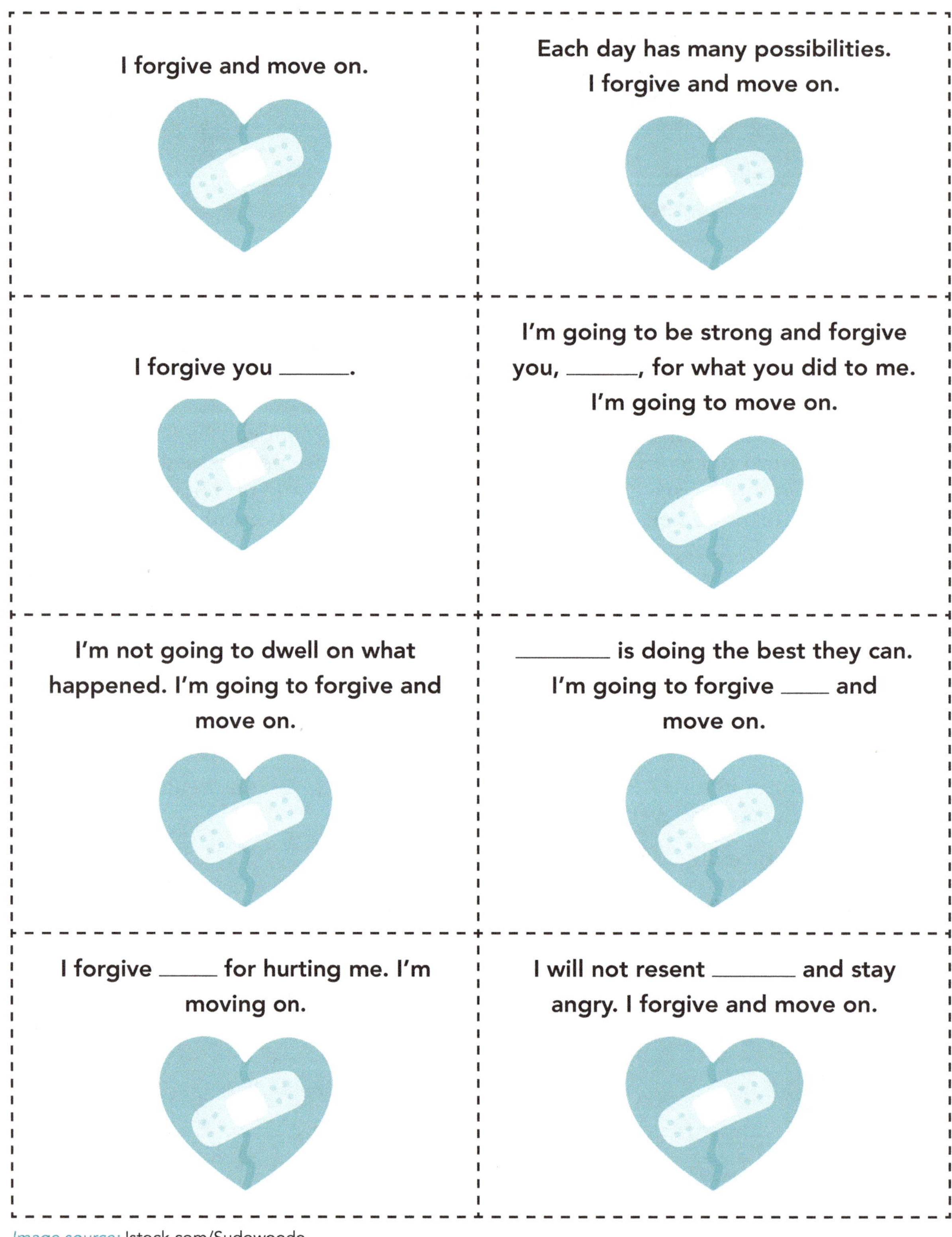

Image source: Istock.com/Sudowoodo

Readers who would like more information about research supporting these intervention strategies can consult the Part IV references listed at the end of the book.

REFERENCES

Introduction

American Academy of Pediatrics. (2022). *Interim guidance on supporting the emotional and behavioral health needs of children, adolescents, and families during the COVID-19 pandemic.* https://www.aap.org/en/pages/2019-novel-coronavirus-covid-19-infections/clinical-guidance/interim-guidance-on-supporting-the-emotional-and-behavioral-health-needs-of-children-adolescents-and-families-during-the-covid-19-pandemic/

Banks, T., & Obiakor, F. E. (2015). Culturally responsive behavior supports: Considerations for practice. *Journal of Education and Training Studies, 3*(2), 83–90. https://doi.org/10.11114/jets.v3i2.636

Bjärehed, M., Thornberg, R., Wänström, L., & Gini, G. (2021). Individual moral disengagement and bullying among Swedish fifth graders: The role of collective moral disengagement and pro-bullying behavior within classrooms. *Journal of Interpersonal Violence, 36*(17–18), NP9576-NP9600. https://doi.org/10.1177/0886260519860888

Black, D. S., & Fernando, R. (2014). Mindfulness training and classroom behavior among lower-income and ethnic minority elementary school children. *Journal of Child and Family Studies, 23*(7), 1242–1246. https://doi.org/10.1007/s10826-013-9784-4

Bronstein, B., Breeden, N., Glover, T. A., & Reddy, L. A. (2021). Paraprofessionals' perceptions of behavior problems in elementary school classrooms. *The Journal of Special Education, 55*(3), 153–162. doi: https:/10.1177/002246692096108

Campos, D., & Fad, K. M. (2023). *Help anxious kids in a stressful world: 25 classroom strategies.* Free Spirit Publishing.

Center of Multi-Tiered System of Supports. (2024). *Multi-Level prevention system.* https://mtss4success.org/essential-components/multi-level-prevention-system

EAB District Leadership Forum. (2019). *Breaking bad behavior. The rise of classroom disruptions in early grades and how districts are responding.* EAB Global, Inc. https://pages.eab.com/rs/732-GKV-655/images/BreakingBadBehaviorStudy.pdf

EAB Executive Briefing. (2023). *Building a better behavior management strategy for students and teachers. Key findings from EAB's student behavior survey*. EAB Global, Inc. https://pages.eab.com/rs/732-GKV-655/images/Student%20Behavior%20Executive%20Briefing.pdf

EAB Press Release. (2023, Feb. 16). *Two new EAB surveys reveal troubling trends in student behavior.* EAB Global, Inc. https://eab.com/about/newsroom/press/two-new-eab-surveys-reveal-troubling-trends-in-student-behavior/#:~:text=Two%20New%20EAB%20Surveys%20Reveal%20Troubling%20Trends%20in%20Student%20Behavior,-Twice%20as%20many&text=SAN%20ANTONIO%2C%20Texas%2C%20(February,students%20prior%20to%20the%20pandemic

Fad, K. M., & Campos, D. (2021). *Lonely kids in a connected world: What teachers can do. Grades 3–8.* Ancora Publishing.

Hamsho, N. F., & Eckert, T. L. (2021). The relation between classroom behaviors and the writing skills of urban third-grade students. *Reading & Writing Quarterly: Overcoming Learning Difficulties, 37*(2), 190–200. https://doi.org/10.1080/10573569.2020.1796862

Kirkpatrick, M., Rivera, G., & Akers, J. (2022). Systematic review of behavioral interventions using digital technology to reduce problem behavior in the classroom. *Journal of Behavioral Education, 31*(1), 69–53. https://doi.org/10.1007/s10864-020-09406-1

McDaniel, S. C., Bruhn, A. L., & Troughton, L. (2017). A brief social skills intervention to reduce challenging classroom behavior. *Journal of Behavioral Education, 26*(1), 53–74. https://doi.org/10.1007/s10864-016-9259-y

Närhi, V., Kiiski, T., & Savolainen, H. (2017). Reducing disruptive behaviours and improving classroom behavioural climate with class-wide positive behaviour support in middle schools. *British Educational Research Journal, 43*(6), 1186–1205. https://doi.org/10.1002/berj.3305

National Council on Teacher Quality. (2013). *Training our future teachers: Classroom management.* https://www.nctq.org/publications/Training-Our-Future-Teachers:-Classroom-Management

Ratcliff, N. J., Jones, C. R., Costner, R. H., Savage-Davis, E., & Hunt, G. H. (2010). The elephant in the classroom: The impact of misbehavior on classroom climate. *Education, 131*(2), 306–314.

Sheaffer, A. W., Majeika, C. E., Gilmour, A. F., & Wehby, J. H. (2021). Classroom behavior of students with or at risk of EBD: Student gender affects teacher ratings but not direct observations. *Behavioral Disorders, 46*(2), 96–107. https://doi.org/10.1177/01987429209116

Simpson, J. N., Hopkins, S., Eakle, C. D., & Rose, C.A. (2020). Implement today! Behavior management strategies to increase engagement and reduce challenging behaviors in the classroom. *Beyond Behavior, 29*(20), 119–128. https://doi.org/10.1177/10742956209094

Watson, T. L., Skinner, C. H., Skinner, A. L., Cazzell, S., Aspiranti, K. B., Moore, T., & Coleman, M. (2016). Preventing disruptive behavior via classroom management: Validating the color wheel system in kindergarten classrooms. *Behavior Modification, 40*(4), 518–540. https://doi.org/10.1177/0145445515626890.

Yoleri, S. (2013). The effects behavior problems in preschool children have on their school adjustment. *Education, 134*(2), 218–226.

Chapter 1

Al'Uqdah, S., Grant, S., Malone, C. M., McGee, T., & Toldson, I. A. (2015). Impact of community violence on parenting behaviors and children's outcomes. *The Journal of Negro Education, 84*(3), 428–441. https://doi.org/10.7709/jnegroeducation.84.3.0428

Brokamp, S. K., Houtveen, A. M., & van de Grift, W. J. (2019). The relationship among students' reading performance, their classroom behavior, and teacher skills. *The Journal of Educational Research, 112*(1), 1–11. https://doi.org/10.1080/00220671.2017.1411878

Bronstein, B., Breeden, N., Glover, T. A., & Reddy, L. A. (2021). Paraprofessionals' perceptions of behavior problems in elementary school classrooms. *The Journal of Special Education, 55*(3), 153–162. https://doi.org/10.1177/002246692096108

Busacca, M. L., Anderson, A., & Moore, D. W. (2015). Self-management for primary school students demonstrating problem behavior in regular classrooms: Evidence review of single-case design research. *Journal of Behavioral Education, 24*(4), 373–401. https://doi.org/10.1007/s10864-015-9230-3

Caldalerra, P., Larsen, R. A., Williams, L., & Wills, H. P. (2021). Effects of middle school teachers' praise-to-reprimand ratios on students' classroom behavior. *Journal of Positive Interventions, 25*(1), 28–40. https://doi.org/10.1177/10983007211035185

Charles Butt Foundation. (2022). *The 2023 Texas teacher poll: Listening to the educator experience*. https://charlesbuttfdn.org/wp-content/uploads/2023/09/2023-teacher-poll.pdf

Centers for Disease Control and Prevention. (2022, February 25). *Mental health surveillance among children—United States, 2013–2019*. Morbidity and Mortality Weekly Report. https://www.ncbi.nlm.nih.gov/pmc/articles/PMC8890771/pdf/su7102a1.pdf

Darawshy, N. A., Gewirtz, A., & Marsalis, S. (2020). Psychological intervention and prevention programs for child and adolescent exposure to community violence: A systematic review. *Clinical Child and Family Psychology Review, 23*(3), 365–378. https://doi.org/10.1007/s10567-020-00315-3

Dempster, R. M., Wildman, B. G., Langkamp, D., & Duby, J. C. (2012). Pediatrician identification of child behavior problems: The role of parenting factors and cross-practice differences. *Journal of Clinical Psychology in Medical Settings, 19*(2), 177–187. https://doi.org/10.1007/s10880-011-9268-x

Floress, M. T., & Beschta, S. L. (2018). An analysis of general education teachers' use of diverse praise. *Psychology in the Schools, 55*(10), 1188–1204. https://doi.org/10.1002/pits.22187

Hirsch, S. E., Lloyd, J. W., & Kennedy, M. J. (2019). Improving novice teachers' use of universal classroom management. *The Elementary School Journal, 120*(1), 61–87. https://doi.org/10.1086/704492

Hoffman, T. K., & Kuvalanka, K. A. (2019). Behavior problems in child care classrooms: Insights from child care teachers. *Preventing School Failure, 63*(3), 259–268. https://doi.org/10.1080/1045988X.2019.1588215

IRIS Center at Vanderbilt University. (2012). *Defining behavior: Case study unit*. https://iris.peabody.vanderbilt.edu/wp-content/uploads/2013/05/ICS-015.pdf

Kersten, L., Vriends, N., Steppan, M., Raschle, N.M., Praetzlich, M., Oldenhof, H., Vermeiren, R., Jansen, L., Ackermann, K., Bernhard, A., Martinelli, A., Gonzalez-Madruga, K., Puzzo, I., Wells, A., Rogers, J. C., Clanton, R., Baker, R. H., Grisley, L., Baumann, S., . . . Stadler, C. (2017). Community violence exposure and conduct problems in children and adolescents with conduct disorder and healthy controls. *Frontiers in Behavioral Neuroscience, 11*(219), 1–14. https://doi.org/10.3389/fnbeh.2017.00219

Kirkpatrick, M., Rivera, G., & Akers, J. (2022). Systematic review of behavioral interventions using digital technology to reduce problem behavior in the classroom. *Journal of Behavioral Education, 31*(1), 69–53. https://doi.org/10.1007/s10864-020-09406-1

Loona, M. I., & Kamal, A. (2012). Role of parenting styles and familial factors in prediction of teacher-report childhood behavior problems. *Journal of Behavioural Sciences, 32*(3), 678–690. https://doi.org/10.1007/s10826-023-02551-x

Long, A. C., Upright, F. G., & Miller, J. J. (2019). Classroom management for ethnic-racial minority students: A meta-analysis of single-case design studies. *School Psychology Quarterly, 34*(1), 1–13. https://doi.org/10.1037/spq0000305

Mak, M. C., Yin, L., Li, M., Cheung, R. Y., & Oon, P. T. (2020). The relation between parenting stress and child behavior problems: Negative parenting styles as mediator. *Journal of Child and Family Studies, 29*(11), 2993–3003. https://doi.org/10.1007/s10826-020-01785-3

Mohammed, E. T., Shapiro, E. R., Wainwright, L. D., & Carter, A. S. (2015). Impacts of family and community violence exposure on child coping and mental health. *Journal of Abnormal Child Psychology, 43*(2), 203–215. https://doi.org/10.1007/s10802-014-9889-2

Simpson, J. N., Hopkins, S., Eakle, C. D., & Rose, C. A. (2020). Implement today! Behavior management strategies to increase engagement and reduce challenging behaviors in the classroom. *Beyond Behavior, 29*(20), 119–128. https://doi.org/10.1177/1074295 6209094

Stichter, J. P., Lewis, T. J., Whittaker, T. A., Richter, M., Johnson, N. W., & Trussell, R. P. (2009). Assessing teacher use of opportunities to respond and effective classroom management strategies. *Journal of Positive Behavior Intervention, 11*(2), 68–81. https://doi.org/10.1177/109830070832659

Sun, R. C., & Shek, D. T. (2012). Student classroom misbehavior: An exploratory study based on teachers' perceptions. *The Scientific World Journal*, 2012, 1–8. https://doi.org/10.1100/2012/208907

Tomlinson, C. A. (2011). *One to grow on: Respecting students.* Retrieved from https://www.ascd.org/el/articles/respecting-students

Vučković, S., Ručević, S., & Ajduković, M. (2021). Parenting style and practices and children's externalizing behaviour problems: Mediating role of children's executive functions. *European Journal of Developmental Psychology, 18*(3), 313–329.

Weinstein, C. S., Curran, M., & Saundra, T. (2003). Culturally responsive classroom management: Awareness into action. *Classroom Management in a Diverse Society, 43*(4), 269–276.

Yoleri, S. (2013). The effects behavior problems in preschool children have on their school adjustment. *Education, 134*(2), 218–226.

Zoromski, A., Evans, S. W., Owens, J. S., Holdaway, A., & Romero, A. S. (2021). Middle school teachers' perceptions and use of classroom management strategies and associations with student behavior. *Journal of Emotional and Behavioral Disorders, 29*(4), 199–212. https://doi.org/10.1177/1063426620957624

Chapter 2

Allday, R. A. (2018). Functional thinking for managing challenging behavior. *Intervention in School and Clinic, 53*(4), 245–251. https://doi.org/10.1177/10534512177129

Barron, L., & Kinney, P. (2021). *We belong: 50 strategies to create community and revolutionize classroom management.* ASCD.

Billingsley, G. M. (2016). Combating work refusal using research-based practices. *Behavior Management, 52*(1), 12–16. https://doi.org/10.1177/1053451216630289

Caldalerra, P., Larsen, R. A., Williams, L., & Wills, H. P. (2021). Effects of middle school teachers' praise-to-reprimand ratios on students' classroom behavior. *Journal of Positive Interventions, 25*(1), 28–40. https://doi.org/10.1177/10983007211035185

Coy, J. N., & Kostewicz, D. E. (2018). Noncontingent reinforcement: Enriching the classroom environment to reduce problem behaviors. *Teaching Exceptional Children, 50*(5), 301–308. https://doi.org/10.1177/00400599187654

Diperna, J. C., Lei, P., Bellinger, J., & Cheng, W. (2016). Effects of a universal positive classroom behavior program on student learning. *Psychology in the Schools, 53*(2), 189–203. https://doi.org/10.1002/pits.21891

Fallon, L. M., Veiga, M. B., Susilo, A. Robinson-Link, P., Berkman, T. S., Minami, T., & Kilgus, S. P. (2020). Exploring the relationship between teachers' perceptions of cultural responsiveness, student risk, and classroom behavior. *Psychology in the Schools, 59*(10), 1–17. https://doi.org/10.1002/pits.22568

Frieberg, J. H., Huzinec, C. A., & Templeton, S. M. (2009). Classroom management—A pathway to student achievement: A study of fourteen inner-city elementary schools. *Elementary School Journal, 110*(1), 63–80. https://doi.org/10.1086/598843

Herbert-Myers, H., Guttentag, C. L., Swank, P. R., Smith, K. E., & Landry, S. H. (2006). The importance of language, social, and behavioral skills across early and later childhood as predictors of social competence with peers. *Applied Developmental Science, 10*(4), 174–187. https://doi.org/10.1207/s1532480xads1004_2

Hirsch, S. E., Lloyd, J. W., & Kennedy, M. J. (2019). Improving novice teachers' use of universal classroom management. *The Elementary School Journal, 120*(1), 61–87. https://doi.org/10.1086/704492

Lara, L. C. (2020). Benefits of journal-writing for students in the emotional/behavior disorders classroom. *Journal of Poetry Therapy, 33*(3), 187–193. https://doi.org/10.1080/08893675.2020.1776971

Lassiter, J. W., & Campbell, A. L. (2019). Effect of an elementary school walking program on physical activity and classroom behavior. *The Physical Educator, 76*(2), 485–501.

Marzano, R. J., Marzano, J. S., & Pickering, D. J. (2003). *Classroom management that works: Research-based strategies for every teacher.* ASCD.

Moreno, G., & Bullock, L. M. (2011). Principles of positive behaviour supports: Using the FBA as a problem-solving approach to address challenging behaviours beyond special populations. *Emotional and Behavioural Difficulties, 16*(2), 117–127. https://doi.org/10.1080/13632752.2011.569394

National Council on Teacher Quality (NCTQ). (2013, December). *Training our future teachers: Classroom management.* https://www.nctq.org/publications/Training-Our-Future-Teachers:-Classroom-Management

POWER-Solving. (2022). *Benefits of social skills learning.* https://power-solving.com/why-social-sklls/benefits-of-social-skills-learning/

Ratcliff, N. J., Jones, C. R., Costner, R. H., Savage-Davis, E., & Hunt, G. H. (2010). The elephant in the classroom: The impact of misbehavior on classroom climate. *Education, 131*(2), 306–314.

Rimm-Kaufman, S., & Sandilos, L. (2015). *Improving students' relationships with teachers to provide essential supports for learning: Applications of psychological science to teaching and learning modules.* https://www.apa.org/education-career/k12/relationships

Ruef, M. B., Higgins, C., Glaeser, B. J., & Patnode, M. (1998). Positive behavioral support: Strategies for teachers. *Intervention in School and Clinic, 34*(1), 21–32. https://doi.org/10.1177/105345129803400103

Scott, T. M., Nelson, C.M., & Liaupsin, C. J. (2001). Effective instruction: The forgotten component in preventing school violence. *Education and Treatment of Children, 24*(3), 309–322.

Shamnadh, M., & Anzari, A. (2019). Misbehavior of school students in classrooms – Main causes and effective strategies to manage it. *International Journal of Scientific Development and Research, 4*(3), 318–321.

Stichter, J. P., Lewis, T. J., Whittaker, T. A., Richter, M., Johnson, N. W., & Trussell, R. P. (2009). Assessing teacher use of opportunities to respond and effective classroom management strategies. *Journal of Positive Behavior Intervention, 11*(2), 68–81. https://doi.org/10.1177/109830070832659

Chapter 3

Babkie, A. M. (2006). Be proactive in managing classroom behavior. *Intervention in School and Clinic, 41*(3), 184–187. https://doi.org/10.1177/10534512060410031001

Downs, K. R., Caldarella, P. Larsen, R. A., Charlton, C. T., Wills, H. P., Kamps, D. M., & Wehby, J. H. (2019). Teacher praise and reprimands: The differential response of students at risk of emotional and behavioral disorders. *Journal of Positive Behavior Intervention, 21*(3), 135–147. https://doi.org/10.1177/1098300718800824

Fielstein, L., & Phelps, P. (2001). *Introduction to teaching: Rewards and realities.* Wadsworth.

Hirsch, S. E., Lloyd, J. W., & Kennedy, M. J. (2019). Improving novice teachers' use of universal classroom management. *The Elementary School Journal, 120*(1), 61–87. https://doi.org/10.1086/704492

Munson, D. (2000). *Enemy pie.* Chronicle Books.

Närhi, V., Kiiski, T., & Savolainen, H. (2017). Reducing disruptive behaviours and improving classroom behavioural climate with class-wide positive behaviour support in middle schools. *British Educational Research Journal, 43*(6), 1186–1205. https://doi.org/10.1002/berj.3305

Ormrod, J. E., Anderman, E. M., & Anderman, L. H. (2019). *Educational psychology: Developing learners*. Pearson.

Owens, J. S., Holdaway, A. S., Smith, J., Evans, S. W., Himawan, L. K., Coles, E. K., Girio-Herrera, E., Mixon, C. S., Egan, T. E., & Dawson, A. E. (2018). Rates of common classroom behavior management strategies and their associations with challenging student behavior in elementary school. *Journal of Emotional and Behavioral Disorders, 26*(13), 156–169. https://doi.org/10.1177/1063426617712501

Ratcliff, N. J., Jones, C. R., Costner, R. H., Savage-Davis, E., & Hunt, G. H. (2010). The elephant in the classroom: The impact of misbehavior on classroom climate. *Education, 131*(2), 306–314.

Ruef, M. B., Higgins, C., Glaeser, B. J., & Patnode, M. (1998). Positive behavioral support: Strategies for teachers. *Intervention in School and Clinic, 34*(1), 21–32. https://doi.org/10.1177/105345129803400103

Simpson, J. N., Hopkins, S., Eakle, C. D., & Rose, C. A. (2020). Implement today! Behavior management strategies to increase engagement and reduce challenging behaviors in the classroom. *Beyond Behavior, 29*(20), 119–128. https://doi.org/10.1177/10742956209094

Sobeck, E. E., & Reister, M. (2021). Preventing challenging behavior: 10 behavior management strategies every teacher should know. *Preventing school failure: Alternative education for children and youth, 65*(1), 70–78. https://doi.org/10.1080/1045988X.2020.1821347

Whitney, T., & Ackerman, K. B. (2020). Acknowledging student behavior: A review of methods promoting positive and constructive feedback. *Beyond Behavior, 29*(2), 86–94. https://doi.org/10.1177/1074295620902474

Zoromski, A., Evans, S. W., Owens, J. S., Holdaway, A., & Romero, A. S. (2021). Middle school teachers' perceptions and use of classroom management strategies and associations with student behavior. *Journal of Emotional and Behavioral Disorders, 29*(4), 199–212. https://doi.org/10.1177/1063426620957624

Chapter 4

Black, D. S., & Fernando, R. (2014). Mindfulness training and classroom behavior among lower-income and ethnic minority elementary school children. *Journal of Child and Family Studies, 23*(7), 1242–1246. https://doi.org/10.1007/s10826-013-9784-4

Busacca, M. L., Anderson, A., & Moore, D. W. (2015). Self-management for primary school students demonstrating problem behavior in regular classrooms: Evidence review of single-case design research. *Journal of Behavioral Education, 24*(4), 373–401. https://doi.org/10.1007/s10864-015-9230-3

Campos, D., & Fad, K. M. (2023). *Help anxious kids in a stressful world: 25 classroom strategies*. Free Spirit Publishing.

Gray, C. A. (1998). Social stories™ and comic strip conversations with students with Asperger Syndrome and high-functioning autism. In E. Schopler, G. B. Mesibov, & L.J. Kunce (Eds.), *Asperger syndrome or high-functioning autism?* (pp. 167–198). Plenum.

Gray, C. A., & Garand, J. D. (1993). Social stories™: Improving responses of students with autism with accurate social information. *Focus on Autistic Behavior, 8*(1), 1–10.

Johnson, Z. D., Goldman, Z. W., & Claus, C. J. (2019). Why do students misbehave? An initial examination of antecedents to student misbehavior. *Communication Quarterly, 67*(1), 1–20.

McConnell, K., & Synatschk, K. O. (2012). *Positive alternatives to restraint and seclusion for aggressive kids*. PRO-ED.

Schneider, N., & Goldstein, H. (2009). Social stories™ improve the on-task behavior of children with language impairment. *Journal of Early Intervention, 31*(3), 250–264. https://doi.org/10.1177/1053815109339564

Chapter 5

Cooper, J. T., & Scott, T. M. (2017). The keys to managing instruction and behavior: Considering high probability practices. *Teacher Education and Special Education, 40* (2), 102–113. https://doi.org/10.1177/0888406417700825

Floress, M. T., & Beschta, S. L. (2018). An analysis of general education teachers' use of diverse praise. *Psychology in the Schools, 55* (10), 1188–1204.

Franklin, H., & Harrington, I. (2019). A review into effective classroom management and strategies for student engagement: Teacher and student roles in today's classrooms. *Journal of Education and Training Studies, 7*(12), 1–12. https://doi.org/10.11114/jets.v7i12.4491

Guardino, C. A., & Fullerton, E. (2010). Changing behaviors by changing the classroom environment. *TEACHING Exceptional Children, 42*(6), 8–13.

Gunersel, A., Mason, B., Wills, H., Caldarella, P., Williams, L., & Henley, V. (2023). Effective classroom management in middle level schools: A qualitative study of teacher perceptions. *Research in Middle Level Education, 46*(8), 1–13. https://doi.org/10.1080/19404476.2023.2252714

Moore, T. C., Robertson, R. E., Maggin, D. M., Oliver, R. M., & Wehby, J. H. (2010). Using teacher praise and opportunities to respond to promote appropriate student behavior. *Preventing School Failure, 54*(3), 172–178. https://doi.org/10.1080/10459880903493179

O'Connor, K. M., & Hayes, B. (2020). How effective are targeted interventions for externalizing behavior when delivered in primary schools? *International Journal of School & Educational Psychology, 8*(3), 161–173. https://doi.org/10.1080/21683603.2018.1530157

O'Handley, R. D., Olmi, D. J., Dufrene, B. A., Tingstrom, D. H., & Whipple, H. (2020). The effects of behavior-specific praise and public posting in secondary classrooms. *Psychology in the Schools, 57*(7), 1097–1115.

Parsonson, B. S. (2012). Evidence-based classroom behaviour management strategies. *Kairaranga, 13*(1), 16–23.

Perle, J. G. (2018). Teacher-provided positive attending to improve student behavior. *TEACHING Exceptional Children, 50*(4), 204–212. https://doi.org/10.1177/0040059918757954

Riden, B. S., Kumm, S., & Maggin, D. M. (2022). Evidence-based behavior management strategies for students with or at risk of EBD: A mega review of the literature. *Remedial and Special Education, 43*(4), 255–269. https://doi.org/10.1177/07419325211047947

Chapter 6

EAB District Leadership Forum. (2019). *Breaking bad behavior. The rise of classroom disruptions in early grades and how districts are responding.* EAB Global, Inc. https://pages.eab.com/rs/732-GKV-655/images/BreakingBadBehaviorStudy.pdf

EAB Executive Briefing. (2023). *Building a better behavior management strategy for students and teachers. Key findings from EAB's student behavior survey.* EAB Global, Inc. https://pages.eab.com/rs/732-GKV-655/images/Student%20Behavior%20Executive%20Briefing.pdf

EAB Press Release. (2023, Feb. 16). *Two new EAB surveys reveal troubling trends in student behavior.* EAB Global, Inc. https://eab.com/about/newsroom/press/two-new-eab-surveys-reveal-troubling-trends-in-student-behavior/#:~:text=Two%20New%20EAB%20Surveys%20Reveal%20Troubling%20Trends%20in%20Student%20Behavior,-Twice%20as%20many&text=SAN%20ANTONIO%2C%20Texas%2C%20(February,students%20prior%20to%20the%20pandemic.

Greenberg, J., Putman, H., & Walsh, K. (2014). *Training our future teachers: Classroom management.* National Council on Teacher Quality. https://www.nctq.org/dmsView/Future_Teachers_Classroom_Management_NCTQ_Report

Harrison, J. R., Vannest, K., David, J., & Reynolds, C. (2012). Common problem behaviors of children and adolescents in general education classrooms in the United States. *Journal of Emotional and Behavioral Disorders, 20(1),* 55–64. https://doi.org/10.1177/106342661421157

Johnson, H. L., & Fullwood, H. L. (2006). Disturbing behaviors in the secondary classroom: How do general educators perceive problem behaviors? *Journal of Instructional Psychology, 33(1),* 20–39.

Lane, K. L., Oakes, W. P., Ennis, R. P., & Hirsch, S. E. (2014.) Identifying students for secondary and tertiary prevention efforts: How do we determine which students have Tier 2 and Tier 3 needs? *Preventing School Failure, 58(3),* 171–182. https://doi.org/10.1080/1045988X,2014.895573

McConnell, K., Ryser, G. R., & Patton, J. R. (2010). *Practical ideas that really work for students with disruptive, defiant, or difficult behaviors (2nd Edition) preschool through grade 4.* PRO-ED.

National Center for Education Statistics. (2023). Teachers' reports of disruptive behaviors and staff rule enforcement. *The Condition of Education. Chapter 2, Preprimary* student, *elementary, and secondary education section: School crime and safety.* 1–6. https://nces.ed.gov/programs/coe/pdf/2023/A11_508c.pdf

Prothero, A. (2023, April 20). Student behavior isn't getting any better, survey shows. *Education Week.* https://www.edweek.org/leadership/student-behavior-isnt-getting-any-better-survey-shows/2023/04

Sun, R. C., & Shek, D. T. (2012). Student classroom misbehavior: An exploratory study based on teachers' perceptions. *The Scientific World Journal,* 2012, 1–8. https://doi.org/10.1100/2012/208907

Whalen, C., & Moore, A. (2023). *White paper: Preparing educators to address the rising problem of behavior problems.* ReThinkEd. 1–19. https://www.rethinked.com/wp-content/uploads/2023/10/preparing-educators-address-rising-problem-behavior-problems-white-paper-rethinked.pdf

Part IV

Beyond Traditional Math (2016). *5 tips for establishing respectful group work routines.* https://beyondtraditionalmath.com/2016/08/07/5-tips-for-establishing-respectful-group-work-routines/

Campos, D., & Fad, K. M. (2023). *Help anxious kids in a stressful world: 25 classroom strategies.* Free Spirit Publishing.

INDEX

Zeitfracht Medien GmbH
Ferdinand-Jühlke-Straße 7
99095 Erfurt, Deutschland
produktsicherheit@kolibri360.de